10 Apps in 10 Weeks

10 Apps in 10 Weeks

Mark Lassoff

LearnToProgram, Inc.
Vernon, Connecticut

LearnToProgram.tv, Incorporated
27 Hartford Turnpike Suite 206
Vernon, CT 06066
contact@learntoprogram.tv
(860) 840-7090

©2015 by LearnToProgram.tv, Incorporated

ISBN-13: 978-0692412305
ISBN-10: 0692412301

Mark Lassoff, Author and Publisher
Kevin Hernandez, VP/ Production
Alison Downs, Copy Editor
Alexandria O'Brien, Book Layout

Courses Available from LearnToProgram, Inc.

10 Apps in 10 Weeks
3D Fundamentals with iOS
Advanced Javascript Development
AJAX Development
Android Development for Beginners
Become a Certified Web Developer (Level 1)
Become a Certified Web Developer (Level 2)
C Programming for Beginners
C++ for Beginners
Codeless Development with Adobe Muse
Construct 2 for Beginners
Creating a PHP Login Script
CSS Development (with CSS3!)
Design for Coders
Famu.os Javascript Framework
Game Development Fundamentals with Python
Game Development with Python
GitHub Fundamentals
HTML and CSS for Beginners (with HTML5)
HTML5 Mobile App Development with PhoneGap
Introduction to Web Development

iOS Development Code Camp
iOS Development for Beginners Featuring iOS6/7
Java Programming for Beginners
Javascript for Beginners
Joomla for Beginners
jQuery for Beginners
Mobile App Development with HTML5
Mobile Game Development with iOS
Node.js for Beginners
Objective C for Beginners
Photoshop for Coders
PHP & MySQL for Beginners
Programming for Absolute Beginners
Project Management with Microsoft Project
Python for Beginners
Ruby on Rails for Beginners
Swift Language Fundamentals
SQL Database for Beginners
User Experience Design

Books from LearnToProgram, Inc.

Create Your Own MP3 Player with HTML5
CSS Development (with CSS3!)
Game Development with Python
HTML and CSS for Beginners
Javascript for Beginners
PHP and MySQL for Beginners
Programming for Absolute Beginners
Python for Beginners
SQL Database for Beginners
Swift Fundamentals: The Language of iOS Development

The apps shown in this book are part of our extended online course. To access all the downloadable content referenced in this book, please enroll at *https:// LearnToProgram.tv*. Readers get half off the original course value.

10 Apps in 10 Weeks Development Bundle

~~Was: $149~~ | Now: $75 (SAVE 50%)

Coupon Code: **10IN10BOOKDEAL**
Use this coupon code at checkout to apply the Readers' Discount.

Bundle Includes:

- Online Course: **10 Apps in 10 Weeks**
- Bonus Online Course: **Mobile App Development with HTML5**
- Downloadable labs and lab solutions
- Extra downloadable content like game image assets
- Lifetime Access
- 30-Day Money Back Guarantee

Full link: *https://learntoprogram.tv/courses/mobile-development-bundle-10-apps-in-10-weeks-and-mobile-app-development-with-html5?product_id=6825&coupon_code=10IN10BOOKDEAL*

TABLE OF CONTENTS

About the Author:

Mark Lassoff

Mark Lassoff's parents frequently claim that Mark was born to be a programmer. In the mid-eighties when the neighborhood kids were outside playing kickball and throwing snowballs, Mark was hard at work on his Commodore 64 writing games in the BASIC programming language. Computers and programming continued to be a strong interest in college where Mark majored in communication and computer science. Upon completing his college career, Mark worked in the software and web development departments at several large corporations.

In 2001, on a whim, while his contemporaries were conquering the dot com world, Mark accepted a position training programmers in a technical training center in Austin, Texas. It was there that he fell in love with teaching programming.

Teaching programming has been Mark's passion for the last 10 years. Today, Mark is a top technical trainer, traveling the country providing leading courses for software and web developers. Mark's training clients include the Department of Defense, Lockheed Martin, Discover Card Services, and Kaiser Permanente. In addition to traditional classroom training, Mark releases courses on the web, which have been taken by programming students all over the world.

He lives near Hartford, Connecticut where he is in the process of redecorating his condominium.

Welcome

Welcome to 10 Apps in 10 Weeks. During this program you'll create 10 full apps that will work on Apple's iPhone and iPad, Android devices, and Windows mobile devices. Each week you'll create another application— and you'll learn some cool techniques along the way. We'll be using four primary technologies to develop our apps:

HTML: HTML markup is used to build the scaffolding of the application and the user interface.

Javascript: Interactivity is built within the application using the Javascript programming language. The essential logic is coded in Javascript.

jQuery: This Javascript framework is used to style the elements that appear within the user interface.

PhoneGap: Adobe's free PhoneGap library is used to "wrap" the application and make it work the same as native apps across the spectrum of devices.

To do well in this program, you'll likely need some experience with HTML and Javascript. We'll frequently use AJAX techniques to communicate with the server behind the scenes. If you need to review these technologies, we highly recommend that you look into the following LearnToProgram courses:

- HTML and CSS for Beginners (with HTML5)
  (https://learntoprogram.tv/courses/html-css-for-beginners)

- Javascript for Beginners
  (https://learntoprogram.tv/courses/javascript-for-beginners)

- jQuery for Beginners
  (https://learntoprogram.tv/courses/learn-jquery-for-beginners)

- AJAX for Beginners (https://learntoprogram.tv/courses/ajax-tutorial-training)

The most effective way to complete this program is to go week-by-week, developing each application and deploying it to your mobile device. (A mobile device is not required to complete the course, however, as many of the apps can bet tested and demonstrated on your PC or Mac.)

While we do provide complete working copies of each app, you'll likely learn best if you create each application from scratch using the tools that we recommend. By typing in the code yourself (and debugging it!) you'll have a better opportunity to familiarize yourself with the code and become acquainted with the techniques we're using to develop mobile applications.

All of the tools you need to develop mobile applications are free and only a download away. They are all available for both Mac and PC and you'll find they work identically across platforms. Since this is week two, let's quickly go over the tools you'll need to download:

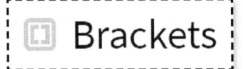

You Need This Now: Brackets

You'll physically write your code in a text editor. Every programmer has a favorite text editor (or two), however, we recommend you use the Brackets text editor, available from www.brackets.io. This tool is actually produced by Adobe and is written in HTML, CSS, and Javascript. You'll find that it gives you plenty of assistance as you develop the application in our 10 week course.

Figure 2-1: The Brackets text editor in action.

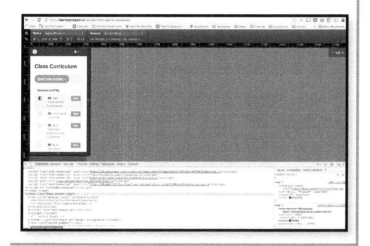

Figure 2-2: The Chrome browser with the developers' tools open (bottom) in mobile emulation mode. Currently the screen of the Apple iPhone 5 is being emulated.

You Need This Now: Chrome

While the apps we create will run in most any browser, for the purpose of testing, I recommend using Google's Chrome browser. Google's Chrome browser has a suite of testing tools that are superior to anything else on the market. Chrome also has an emulation mode that allows you to preview what your app will look like on a mobile device screen. This is an important feature, as you can run out of real estate on a mobile screen much faster than you'd expect.

You Need This Now: PhoneGap

PhoneGap provides the "wrapper" that enables the applications we build in HTML, CSS, and Javascript to run on different mobile device platforms. Installing PhoneGap is a two step process:

1 Visit www.PhoneGap. com and click the "Install" button on the upper right-hand corner of the interface.

2 The installation process is easy. As the install page instructs, make sure you have NodeJS installed. (If you don't, go to www.nodejs.org and click the big green install button.) Next, open your command line and issue the following command as shown in example 2-1.

On a Mac, the command line is accessed through the "terminal" utility. On a PC it can be accessed through the start menu.

The install process can take several minutes and you must have an active internet connection to complete it.

Figure 2-3: The PhoneGap website. The install button appears on the upper right. You may wish to view the helpful intro video provided on the page.

```
sudo npm install -g phonegap
```

Example 2-1: The text command to start the installation.

Really Nice To Have: The PhoneGap Developer App

The PhoneGap Developer App is a somewhat new creation that allows you to bypass the requirements for a developers' license allowing you to test your PhoneGap-wrapped app directly on your device.

To use the PhoneGap Developer App you'll have to install a desktop application on your development system. Then you'll need to download the appropriate mobile app for your iPhone, Android, or Windows device. Next, using your local wireless network, you'll pair the two and you'll be able to test your apps through your mobile device. The PhoneGap Developer App is for testing only and will not help you with deploying your application in an app store.

Nice To Have: Android SDK

If you wish to test your apps on an actual Android device or on the Android emulator you'll need to download the Android software development kit, or SDK. You can download this at http://developer.android.com/sdk/index.html. This is a good time to get a sandwich, as this download and installation can take some time.

Figure 2-4: The Android Studio is used mostly to develop native-style Android apps that aren't compatible with other types of devices.

Nice To Have: Xcode (Mac Only)

If you are planning on testing or releasing on an actual iOS device, be prepared to shell out a hundred bucks for an Apple Developer's license. Once you do, you'll need to download Apple's development environment called Xcode. The Xcode environment itself is free and there you'll be able to provision your iPhone and iPad devices to run your apps.

Figure 2-5: Apple's iOS Development Center. Click the register link to sign up for Apple's iOS Developer program.

MP3 Player Application

This week we're going to create a complete mobile app. As you get ready, you might want to grab a couple of your favorite MP3s, as you'll likely be hearing them over and over again as you complete this tutorial.

This application is going to be developed using four technologies:

HTML: HTML markup is used to build the scaffolding of the application and the user interface.

Javascript: Interactivity is built within the application using the Javascript programming language. The essential logic is coded in Javascript.

jQuery: This Javascript framework is used to style the elements that appear within the user interface.

PhoneGap: Adobe's free PhoneGap library is used to "wrap" the application and make it work the same as native apps across the spectrum of devices.

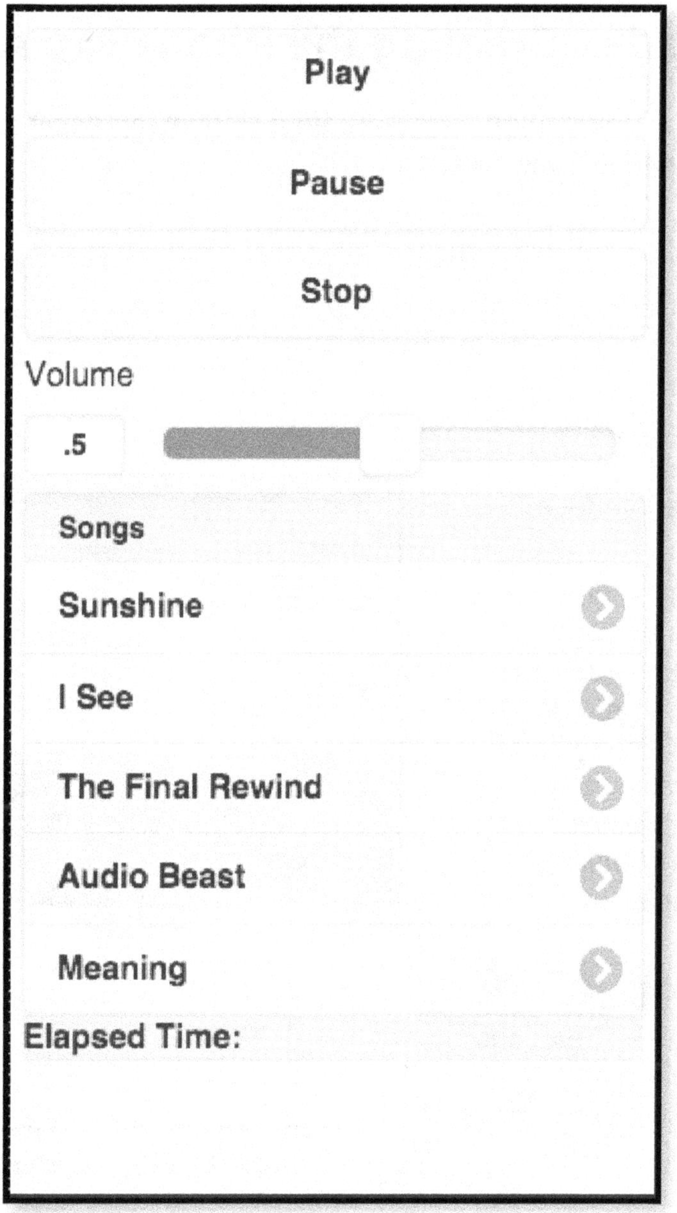

Figure 1-1: MP3 Player Mobile Application User interface developed in HTML, CSS, Javascript and jQuery Mobile.

Getting Ready - Creating the PhoneGap Application

In this initial section of the tutorial we'll create a PhoneGap application and modify the template provided for our own use.

1 Visit www.PhoneGap.com and click the "Install" button on the upper right-hand corner of the interface.

2 The installation process is easy. As the install page instructs, make sure you have NodeJS installed. (If you don't, go to www.nodejs.org and click the big green install button.) Next, open your command line and issue the command specified in example 1-1.

On a Mac, the command line is accessed through the "terminal" utility. On a PC it can be accessed through the start menu.

The install process can take several minutes and you must have an active internet connection to complete it.

Figure 1-2: The PhoneGap website. The install button appears on the upper right. You may wish to view the helpful intro video provided on the page.

```
sudo npm install -g phonegap
```

Example 1-1: The terminal command to install PhoneGap.

3 With PhoneGap installed, we'll now create the PhoneGap Template app. When you create a new PhoneGap application, a template app is installed by PhoneGap. This template is essentially a placeholder and most of it can be removed. To create the PhoneGap app, make sure your command line is pointed at the location where you want to save the app. I used the desktop. (You can use the **cd** command on the command line to change directories on Mac and PC.) Issue the command shown in example 1-2 to create the PhoneGap template app.

▸ `phonegap create musicPlayer`

Example 1-2: The terminal command to create the new PhoneGap application.

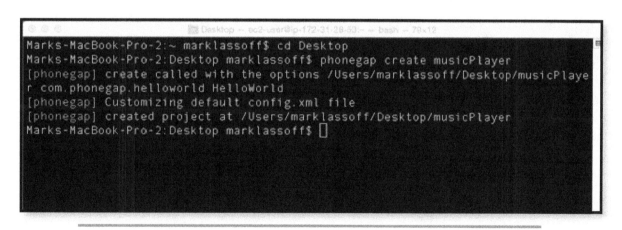

Figure 1-3: Command line after create template application.

④ The command you issued created a folder called musicPlayer. Open that folder and then the **www** folder inside it. Inside that folder, delete everything except config.xml and index.html. The files and folders we're deleting are for the template application that we don't need.

⑤ Open index.html in your text editor. There are references to the template application in the code that we don't need. Edit your code so it appears as shown in example 1-3.

⑥ The basic template in example 1-3 can be used for any application. Let's add a little HTML and CSS to create a container for our UI. I like using a container because it makes layout easier. We're going to be adding just a few lines of code. Inside the body tag, add the code shown in example 1-4.

```html
<!DOCTYPE html>
<html>
  <head>
    <meta charset="utf-8" />
    <meta name="format-detection" content="telephone=no" />
    <meta name="msapplication-tap-highlight" content="no" />
    <!-- WARNING: for iOS 7, remove the width=device-width and height=device-height attributes. See https://issues.apache.org/jira/browse/CB-4323 -->
    <meta name="viewport" content="user-scalable=no, initial-scale=1, maximum-scale=1, minimum-scale=1, width=device-width, height=device-height, target-densitydpi=device-dpi" />
    <title>Hello World</title>
    <script type="text/javascript" src="cordova.js"></script>
  </head>
  <body>

  </body>
</html>
```

Example 1-3: The edited template application.

```html
<div id="container">
</div> <!-- container -->
```

Example 1-4: Adding a container to our code.

```
<style>
#container
    {
        margin: 6px;
    }
</style>
```

Example 1-5: Adding some space around the margins of the screen.

7 Next we'll add the CSS to format the container. We'll add some spacing around the margins of the screen to make everything appear more cleanly. Add the code shown in example 1-5 right before the closing head tag.

```
1  <!DOCTYPE html>
2  <html>
3      <head>
4          <meta charset="utf-8" />
5          <meta name="format-detection" content="telephone=no" />
6          <meta name="msapplication-tap-highlight" content="no" />
7          <!-- WARNING: for iOS 7, remove the width=device-width and height=device-height attributes.
   See https://issues.apache.org/jira/browse/CB-4323 -->
8          <meta name="viewport" content="user-scalable=no, initial-scale=1, maximum-scale=1, minimum-
   scale=1, width=device-width, height=device-height, target-densitydpi=device-dpi" />
9          <title>Hello World</title>
10         <script type="text/javascript" src="cordova.js"></script>
11         <style>
12             #container
13                 {
14                     margin: 6px;
15                 }
16         </style>
17     </head>
18     <body>
19         <div id="container">
20         </div> <!-- container -->
21     </body>
22 </html>
23
```

Figure 1-4: Code so far in the Brackets editor.

Creating the User Interface

We're going to use jQuery Mobile to style our user interface (UI). We're going to add the code to connect to the jQuery Mobile library and the HTML to display the user interface. You'll notice the HTML embeds attributes designed to style the components with the jQuery library.

1   Right after the title tag, add the three lines of code as shown in example 1-6.

HINT: Visit http://jquerymobile. com/download/ and you can copy and paste the code from there.

2   The code shown in example 1-6 connects to the necessary jQuery scripts and CSS via a fast content delivery network. Now we'll use jQuery and HTML to create our user interface. You'll insert the code show in example 1-7 inside the container created earlier in the tutorial.

```
<link rel="stylesheet" href="http://code.
jquery.com/mobile/1.4.5/jquery.mobile-
1.4.5.min.css" />
    <script src="http://code.jquery.com/
jquery-1.11.1.min.js"></script>
    <script src="http://code.jquery.com/
mobile/1.4.5/jquery.mobile-1.4.5.min.
js"></script>
```

Example 1-6: Adding code to connect to the jQuery Mobile library.

```
<audio id="player"/>
        <source src="assets/sunshine.mp3" />
        <source src="assets/sunshine.ogg" />
    </audio>
    <button id="btnPlay">Play</button>
    <button id="btnPause">Pause</button>
    <button id="btnStop">Stop</button>
    <label for="rngVolume">Volume</label>
    <input type="range" id="rngVolume" min="0" max="1" step=".01" value='.5'
data-highlight="true" onchange="changeVolume()"/>
    <ul data-role="listview" data-inset="true">
      <li data-role="list-divider">Songs</li>
      <li><a href="#" onclick="changeSong('sunshine')">Sunshine</a></li>
      <li><a href="#" onclick="changeSong('iSee')">I See</a></li>
      <li><a href="#" onclick="changeSong('finalRewind')">The Final Rewind</a></
li>
      <li><a href="#" onclick="changeSong('audioBeast')">Audio Beast</a></li>
      <li><a href="#" onclick="changeSong('meaning')">Meaning</a></li>
    </ul>
    <div data-role="footer">
        <output id="timeOut">Elapsed Time:</output>
    </div>
```

Example 1-7: The code you will insert inside the container created earlier.

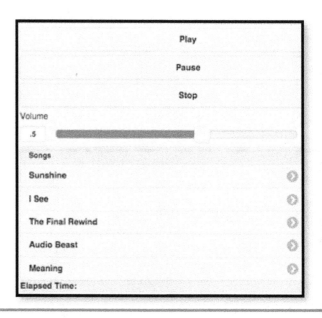

Figure 1-5: Testing the UI in the browser.

③ This is a good place to stop and view our work so far in a web browser. Load the **index. html** from the www folder in to the web browser. Your UI should appear like figure 1-5.

④ If your UI doesn't appear as figure 1-5 shows, check your code and ensure it's correct. There is a complete code listing at the end of this tutorial. If you're using Google's Chrome browser, you can view the UI as it might appear on various mobile devices. Open Chrome's Developer tools by clicking View → Developer → Developer Tools from the dropdown menus.

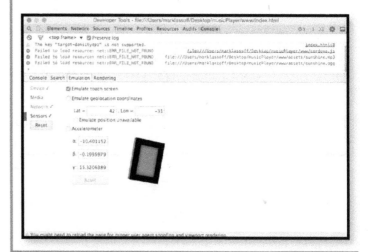

Figure 1-6: Chrome Developer Tools. Choose **Console** from the menu at the top and **Emulation** from the tabs below the log.

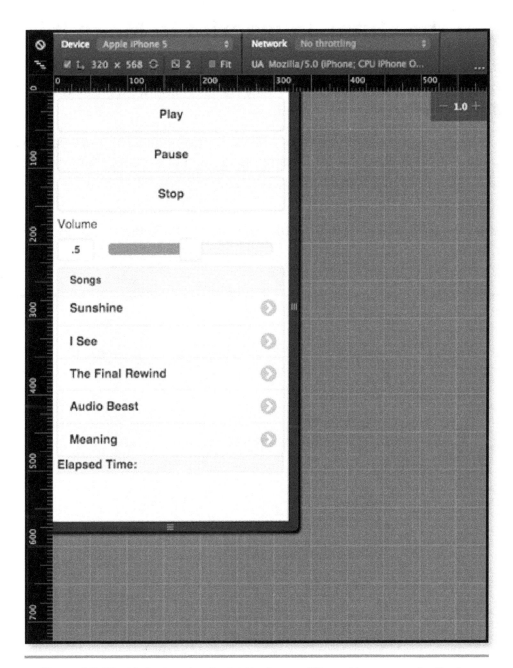

Figure 1-7: The UI displayed as it might look on an iPhone. You can use the **Device** dropdown to choose a specific device you'd like to emulate.

Adding the Guts: Javascript to Make it Work

In this final section of the tutorial, we'll add the necessary Javascript code to make the MP3 player work. Enter the code exactly as listed and we'll break down the code and explain the various sections in a bit.

It's also probably a good time to add our MP3s to the project. (If more convenient for you, you may download the MP3 samples used in this lesson here: https://s3.amazonaws.com/promotionaldownloads/MusicAssets.zip.)

 Enter the following code right after your closing style tag in the document head.

```
<script>
    var player;
    var rngVolume;
    var intv;

    window.onload = function()
    {
      init();
      //document.addEventListener('deviceready', init, false);
    }

    function init()
    {
        player = document.getElementById('player');
        var btnPlay = document.getElementById('btnPlay');
        var btnStop = document.getElementById('btnStop');
        var btnPause = document.getElementById('btnPause');
        rngVolume = document.getElementById('rngVolume');

        btnPlay.addEventListener('click', playMusic, false);
        btnStop.addEventListener('click', stopMusic, false);
        btnPause.addEventListener('click', pauseMusic, false);

    }
```

```
function changeVolume()
{
  player.volume = rngVolume.value;
}

function pauseMusic()
{
  player.pause();
}

function playMusic()
{
  player.play();
  startTimer();
}

function stopMusic()
{
  player.pause();
  player.currentTime = 0;
  stopTimer();
}

function changeSong(song)
{
  stopTimer();
  player.pause();
  player.src = "assets/" + song + ".mp3";
  player.play();
  startTimer();
}

function startTimer()
{
  intv = setInterval(updateTime, 1000);
}

function stopTimer()
{
  clearInterval(intv);
}
```

```
        function updateTime()
        {
          document.getElementById('timeOut').innerHTML = "Elapsed Time: " +
    secsToMins(player.currentTime);
        }

        function secsToMins(seconds)
        {
          var minutes = Math.floor(seconds/60);
          var theSeconds = seconds - minutes * 60;
          if(theSeconds > 9){
            return minutes + ":" + Math.round(theSeconds);
          } else
          {
            return minutes + ":0" + Math.round(theSeconds);
          }


        }
      </script>
```

Example 1-8: Adding some Javascript to make the MP3 player work.

2 Inside your www folder, create a folder called "assets." This folder will hold our MP3s.

3 Inside the assets folder, place the MP3 files. If you use the sample files I've provided, no further changes are needed. If you use your own files, you'll need to replace the names of the songs and files in the HTML. There are a number of lines in the HTML that look like example 1-9.

```
    <li><a href="#"
    onclick="changeSong('sunshine')">Sunshine</
    a></li>
```

Example 1-9: Look through the code and change the name of the songs as needed.

4   If changing the MP3s, inside the changeSong() function, replace the filename "sunshine" with the name of your file. Don't add the .mp3 extension—that's taken care of in the Javascript. You'll also want to change the name of the song displayed before the closing <a>nchor tag. Once you've changed your file names (if you're not using the samples provided) it's time to test your player.

5   Once again, load your index.html file in to the browser. Press play and listen to that sweet music!

6   Test all the features of your MP3 player. If they don't work correctly (or at all), review the code below and see where you made an error.

Congratulations—you've developed a full mobile app!

Understanding the Code

If you're somewhat new to coding, you may find certain sections of the Javascript a bit difficult to follow. We're going to assume foundational HTML and Javascript knowledge here, as we review more difficult sections of the code and explain exactly what they do.

```
window.onload = function()
    {
        init();
        //document.
addEventListener('deviceready', init,
false);
    }
```

Example 1-10: The window.onload function.

1 The function shown in example 1-10 launches once the controls are drawn within the window. The window.onload event is triggered by the browser— or in this case, the browser embedded in PhoneGap. I have commented out the line that activates the PhoneGap deviceready event so that the init() function launches immediately. This allows for browser-based testing as there is no 'deviceready' event outside the PhoneGap environment.

2 Our initialization function (shown in example 1-11) first makes references for the relevant items in the UI, like the buttons and volume slider. 'Click' events are added to the buttons so that they launch the appropriate methods when clicked.

```
    function init()
    {
        player = document.
getElementById('player');
        var btnPlay = document.
getElementById('btnPlay');
        var btnStop = document.
getElementById('btnStop');
        var btnPause = document.
getElementById('btnPause');
        rngVolume = document.
getElementById('rngVolume');

        btnPlay.addEventListener('click',
playMusic, false);
        btnStop.addEventListener('click',
stopMusic, false);
        btnPause.addEventListener('click',
pauseMusic, false);

    }
```

Example 1-11: The initialization function.

```
        function changeVolume()
        {
          player.volume = rngVolume.value;
        }

        function pauseMusic()
        {
          player.pause();
        }

        function playMusic()
        {
          player.play();
          startTimer();
        }

        function stopMusic()
        {
          player.pause();
          player.currentTime = 0;
          stopTimer();
        }
```

Example 1-12: Additional functions that make adjustments to the UI controls possible.

```
        function changeSong(song)
        {
          stopTimer();
          player.pause();
          player.src = "assets/" + song +
   ".mp3";
          player.play();
          startTimer();
        }
```

Example 1-13: The Javascript function to change the song.

3 You can almost determine what these functions do from context. Triggered by the controls on the UI, these functions make actual adjustments to the status of the audio feed by changing the volume or pausing the music. You'll notice that there is no stop() function for the audio— only pause. To stop we have to pause and reset the playhead to the beginning of the audio clip.

4 When the user clicks a different song on the player we have to stop the timer, pause the current song, and change the src attribute of the player to point to the appropriate audio file. After that process the player is restarted (now playing the new song) and the timer is started again.

5 Code example 1-14 shows functions that all deal with managing the timer. When the timer is started in the startTimer() function, an interval is created to call the updateTime() function once per second. updateTime() replaces the timer output. The secsToMins() function changes the seconds into minutes and seconds in a format readable by humans.

```
        function startTimer()
        {
            intv = setInterval(updateTime,
    1000);
        }

        function stopTimer()
        {
            clearInterval(intv);
        }

        function updateTime()
        {
            document.getElementById('timeOut').
    innerHTML = "Elapsed Time: " +
    secsToMins(player.currentTime);
        }

        function secsToMins(seconds)
        {
            var minutes = Math.
    floor(seconds/60);
            var theSeconds = seconds - minutes
    * 60;
            if(theSeconds > 9){
                return minutes + ":" + Math.
    round(theSeconds);
            } else
            {
                return minutes + ":0" + Math.
    round(theSeconds);
            }

        }
```

Example 1-14: These functions deal with the timer.

Testing on a Device

The easiest way to test on an actual device is to use the new PhoneGap Developer app which is free and available on the PhoneGap website.

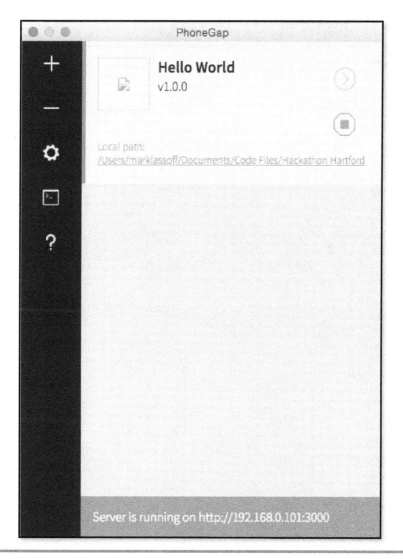

Figure 1-8: The PhoneGap developer application is available from app.phonegap.com

Once you download the app to your development computer and the associated iOS, Android, or Windows mobile app, you'll be able to test your PhoneGap apps on your device without a cumbersome installation process.

For your reference, here's the full code for the MP3 player:

MP3 Player Code Listing

```
<!DOCTYPE html>
<html>
  <head>
    <meta charset="utf-8" />
    <meta name="format-detection" content="telephone=no" />
    <meta name="msapplication-tap-highlight" content="no" />
    <!-- WARNING: for iOS 7, remove the width=device-width and height=device-height
attributes. See https://issues.apache.org/jira/browse/CB-4323 -->
    <meta name="viewport" content="user-scalable=no, initial-scale=1, maximum-
scale=1, minimum-scale=1, width=device-width, height=device-height, target-
densitydpi=device-dpi" />
    <link rel="stylesheet" href="http://code.jquery.com/mobile/1.4.5/jquery.mobile-
1.4.5.min.css" />
    <script src="http://code.jquery.com/jquery-1.11.1.min.js"></script>
    <script src="http://code.jquery.com/mobile/1.4.5/jquery.mobile-1.4.5.min.js"></
script>
    <script type="text/javascript" src="cordova.js"></script>
    <style>
      #container
      {
        margin: 6px;
      }
    </style>
    <script>
      var player;
      var rngVolume;
      var intv;

      window.onload = function()
      {
        init();
        //document.addEventListener('deviceready', init, false);
      }
```

```
function init()
    {
        player = document.getElementById('player');
        var btnPlay = document.getElementById('btnPlay');
        var btnStop = document.getElementById('btnStop');
        var btnPause = document.getElementById('btnPause');
        rngVolume = document.getElementById('rngVolume');

        btnPlay.addEventListener('click', playMusic, false);
        btnStop.addEventListener('click', stopMusic, false);
        btnPause.addEventListener('click', pauseMusic, false);

    }

    function changeVolume()
    {
      player.volume = rngVolume.value;
    }

    function pauseMusic()
    {
      player.pause();
    }

    function playMusic()
    {
      player.play();
      startTimer();
    }

    function stopMusic()
    {
      player.pause();
      player.currentTime = 0;
      stopTimer();
    }

    function changeSong(song)
    {
```

```
                stopTimer();
        player.pause();
        player.src = "assets/" + song + ".mp3";
        player.play();
        startTimer();
    }

    function startTimer()
    {
      intv = setInterval(updateTime, 1000);
    }

    function stopTimer()
    {
      clearInterval(intv);
    }

    function updateTime()
    {
        document.getElementById('timeOut').innerHTML = "Elapsed Time: " +
secsToMins(player.currentTime);
    }

    function secsToMins(seconds)
    {
      var minutes = Math.floor(seconds/60);
      var theSeconds = seconds - minutes * 60;
      if(theSeconds > 9){
        return minutes + ":" + Math.round(theSeconds);
      } else
      {
        return minutes + ":0" + Math.round(theSeconds);
      }

    }
  </script>
  <title>Audio Video</title>
</head>
<body>
  <div id="container">
    <audio id="player"/>
```

```
<source src="assets/sunshine.mp3" />
        <source src="assets/sunshine.ogg" />
    </audio>
    <button id="btnPlay">Play</button>
    <button id="btnPause">Pause</button>
    <button id="btnStop">Stop</button>
    <label for="rngVolume">Volume</label>
    <input type="range" id="rngVolume" min="0" max="1" step=".01" value='.5'
data-highlight="true" onchange="changeVolume()"/>
    <ul data-role="listview" data-inset="true">
      <li data-role="list-divider">Songs</li>
      <li><a href="#" onclick="changeSong('sunshine')">Sunshine</a></li>
      <li><a href="#" onclick="changeSong('iSee')">I See</a></li>
      <li><a href="#" onclick="changeSong('finalRewind')">The Final Rewind</a></li>
      <li><a href="#" onclick="changeSong('audioBeast')">Audio Beast</a></li>
      <li><a href="#" onclick="changeSong('meaning')">Meaning</a></li>
    </ul>
    <div data-role="footer">
        <output id="timeOut">Elapsed Time:</output>
    </div>
  </div><!-- container -->

  </body>
</html>
```

Example 1-15: The finished code for the MP3 player application.

Chuck Norris Joke Generator

Who doesn't love a good Chuck Norris joke? Even the 74-year-old Karate grandmaster is said to laugh at Chuck Norris jokes— before he chops the joke-teller in half, of course.

This week we're going to create a complete mobile app that generates Chuck Norris jokes. Instead of creating a native app that works only on Android or iOS, we're going to create an HTML5-based app that works across multiple platforms.

Getting Ready - Creating the PhoneGap Application

In this initial section of the tutorial we'll create a PhoneGap application and modify the template provided for our own use.

```
▸   phonegap create chuckNorris
```

Example 2-1: The command to create a template app called "chuckNorris."

```
●  ●  ●                    Desktop — bash — 80×24
Last login: Fri Jan 30 08:30:28 on console
Mark-MacBook-Pro:~ marklassoff$ cd Desktop/
Mark-MacBook-Pro:Desktop marklassoff$ phonegap create chuckNorris
Creating a new cordova project with name "Hello World" and id "com.phonegap.hell
oworld" at location "/Users/marklassoff/Desktop/chuckNorris"

Using custom www assets from https://github.com/phonegap/phonegap-app-hello-worl
d/archive/master.tar.gz

Mark-MacBook-Pro:Desktop marklassoff$ ▯
```

Figure 2-1: Command line after create template application.

1   With PhoneGap installed, we'll now create the PhoneGap Template app. When you create a new PhoneGap application, a template app is installed by PhoneGap. This template is essentially a placeholder and most of it can be removed. To create the PhoneGap app, make sure your command line is pointed at the location where you want to save the app. I used the desktop. (You can use the **cd** command on the command line to change directories on Mac and PC.) Issue the command shown in example 2-1 to create the PhoneGap template app.

2 The command you issued created a folder called chuckNorris. Open that folder and then the **www** folder inside it. Inside that folder, delete everything except config.xml and index.html. The files and folders we're deleting are for the template application that we don't need.

3 Open index.html in your text editor. There are references to the template application in the code that we don't need. Edit your code so it appears as shown in example 2-2.

4 The basic template above can be used for any application. Let's add a little HTML and CSS to create a container for our UI. I like using a container because it makes layout easier. We're going to be adding just a few lines of code. Inside the body tag, add the code shown in example 2-3.

```html
<!DOCTYPE html>
<html>
  <head>
    <meta charset="utf-8" />
    <meta name="format-detection"
content="telephone=no" />
    <meta name="msapplication-tap-
highlight" content="no" />
    <!-- WARNING: for iOS 7, remove the
width=device-width and height=device-
height attributes. See https://issues.
apache.org/jira/browse/CB-4323 -->
    <meta name="viewport" content="user-
scalable=no, initial-scale=1, maximum-
scale=1, minimum-scale=1, width=device-
width, height=device-height, target-
densitydpi=device-dpi" />
    <title>Hello World</title>
    <script type="text/javascript"
src="cordova.js"></script>
  </head>
  <body>

  </body>
</html>
```

Example 2-2: The basic code structure that can be used for any application.

```html
<div id="container">
</div> <!-- container -->
```

Example 2-3: Adding a container for the UI.

```
<style>
#container
    {
        margin: 6px;
    }
</style>
```

Example 2-4: Adding some CSS to formate the container.

5   Next we'll add the CSS to format the container. We'll add some spacing around the margins of the screen to make everything appear more cleanly. Add the code shown in example 2-4 right before the closing head tag.

```
1  <!DOCTYPE html>
2  <html>
3      <head>
4          <meta charset="utf-8" />
5          <meta name="format-detection" content="telephone=no" />
6          <meta name="msapplication-tap-highlight" content="no" />
7          <!-- WARNING: for iOS 7, remove the width=device-width and height=device-height attributes.
   See https://issues.apache.org/jira/browse/CB-4323 -->
8          <meta name="viewport" content="user-scalable=no, initial-scale=1, maximum-scale=1, minimum-
   scale=1, width=device-width, height=device-height, target-densitydpi=device-dpi" />
9          <title>Hello World</title>
10         <script type="text/javascript" src="cordova.js"></script>
11         <style>
12             #container
13             {
14                 margin: 6px;
15             }
16         </style>
17     </head>
18     <body>
19         <div id="container">
20         </div> <!-- container -->
21     </body>
22 </html>
23
```

Figure 2-2: Code so far in the Brackets editor.

⑥ To add some simple styling, we're going to include the jQuery mobile libraries. By simply adding the libraries, our user interface will appear more mobile-friendly and attractive. If you point your browser to http://jquerymobile. com/download/ you will find the lines of code below. You can paste them directly into your code, above the <style> element.

```
<link rel="stylesheet" href="http://code.
jquery.com/mobile/1.3.2/jquery.mobile-
1.3.2.min.css" />
    <script src="http://code.jquery.com/
jquery-1.9.1.min.js"></script>
    <script src="http://code.jquery.com/
mobile/1.3.2/jquery.mobile-1.3.2.min.
js"></script>
```

Example 2-5: Adding a mobile-friendly jQuery library.

Creating the User Interface

The Chuck Norris Joke generator app has a very simple interface. Aside from the app title, there is a "Get Joke" button and some instructions. What you can't see is a hidden div that will display the joke when it's received from the server.

If you want to improve this user interface, you can use jQuery's "themeroller" tools to add color and effects to the interface items. See http://themeroller.jquerymobile.com/.

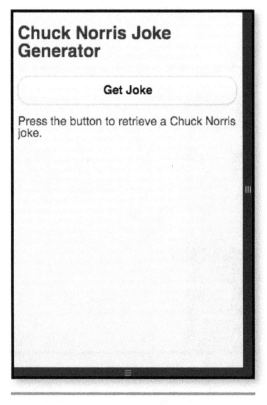

Figure 2-3: Chuck Norris Joke app user interface.

```
<div id="container">
    <h2>Chuck Norris Joke Generator</h2>
    <button id="btnGetJoke">Get Joke</
button>
    <p>Press the button to retrieve a
Chuck Norris joke.</p>
    <div id="joke"></div>
</div> <!-- container -->
```

Example 2-6: Creating the user interface with some HTML.

Believe it or not, only a few lines of code create the user interface.

Once you create the user interface by typing the HTML into the body section of your document, see how it looks in your web browser. If you're using Chrome, you can open the Developer's Tools and use the mobile emulation options to see how the UI would look in an actual mobile device. If your user interface doesn't look like the screen capture above, carefully check your code for bugs.

Adding the Guts: Javascript to Make it Work

We'll add the Javascript all at once in a <script> element in the head of the document. The Javascript, of course, is where the action is, and it is what makes our application actually work. Be careful as you key in the Javascript as a single incorrect keystroke can cause the entire code block not to function. Looking for bugs can be frustrating— but it's a critical part of learning to code.

Here's the Javascript:

```
<script>
    var xmlhttp;

    window.onload=function()
    {
      document.addEventListener("deviceready", init, false);
      //init();
    }

    function init()
    {
      document.getElementById('btnGetJoke').addEventListener('click', getJoke,
false);
      xmlhttp = new XMLHttpRequest();
      xmlhttp.onreadystatechange = receiveJoke;
    }

    function getJoke()
    {
      xmlhttp.open('GET', 'http://api.icndb.com/jokes/random/', false);
      xmlhttp.send();
    }

    function receiveJoke()
    {
      if(xmlhttp.readyState==4 && xmlhttp.status==200)
      {
        var json = jQuery.parseJSON(xmlhttp.responseText);
        // console.log(json);
        document.getElementById('joke').innerHTML = json.value.joke;
      }
    }

    </script>
```

Example 2-7: The Javascript required to complete the application (for now.)

Once you've added the code as shown in example 2-7, the application is complete (for now) and should function. Test this app using The PhoneGap Developer App, not your web browser. Due to cross-site scripting restrictions, most browsers won't receive the JSON code that contains the joke.

Once you get everything working you should see a joke appear below the instructions each time you press the "Get Joke" button.

```
window.onload=function()
    {
        document.
addEventListener("deviceready", init.
false);
        //init();
    }

    function init()
    {
        document.
getElementById('btnGetJoke').
addEventListener('click'. getJoke. false);
        xmlhttp = new XMLHttpRequest();
        xmlhttp.onreadystatechange =
receiveJoke;
    }
```

Example 2-8: Adding the "deviceready" event to initialize the device, the PhoneGap library, and the UI.

```
function getJoke()
    {
        xmlhttp.open('GET', 'http://api.
icndb.com/jokes/random/', false);
        xmlhttp.send();
    }
```

Example 2-9: The function to add a click listener.

Understanding the Code

1 The code (in example 2-7) initializes the functions shown in example 2-8.

The purpose of these functions is to initialize the device, the PhoneGap library and the UI. The initial function simply listens for the "deviceready" event which indicates that the phone (or tablet) is ready to proceed. Once the device is ready, the init() function is run.

2 This function (shown in example 2-9) first adds a click listener to the button. When the button is clicked, the getJoke() function will be run. In the last two lines of initialization, the XMLHttpRequest() object is initialized and receiveJoke() is assigned to deal with the information that comes back from the server.

The getJoke() function, run when the button is pressed, contacts the Chuck Norris joke server and requests a joke. You can point your browser to http://api.icndb.com/jokes/random/ and view how the server responds.

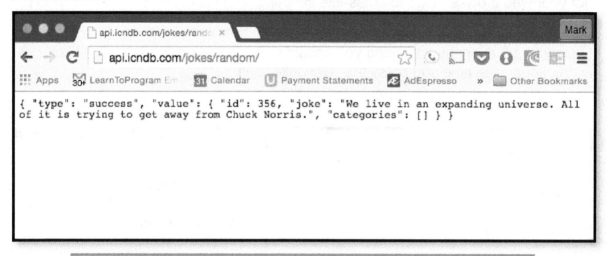

{ "type": "success", "value": { "id": 356, "joke": "We live in an expanding universe. All of it is trying to get away from Chuck Norris.", "categories": [] } }

Figure 2-4: The server responds with JSON notation. You can see the joke embedded in the JSON notation.

3 When the joke is received, the function shown in example 2-10 is run.

This function first ensures that the data sent back from the server indicates a readyState of 4 (server communication complete) and an http response code of 200 (ok).

It then takes the JSON text that has been received by the server and extracts it by its key, "joke." Finally, it displays the joke in the div called joke towards the bottom of the application.

```
function receiveJoke()
    {
        if(xmlhttp.readyState==4 && xmlhttp.status==200)
        {
            var json = jQuery.parseJSON(xmlhttp.responseText);
            // console.log(json);
            document.getElementById('joke').innerHTML = json.value.joke;
        }
    }
```

Example 2-10: This function processes the "readyState."

Testing on a Device

Assuming your device is connected to your computer via USB cable and correctly provisioned (iOS only) you should be able to actually test on your device itself.

If you were testing on an Android device, you should be able to navigate to your project folder using the command line. Once pointed at the project folder, issue the following command:

```
phonegap build android
```

Or, to build on iOS:

```
phonegap build ios
```

If you have the Android SDK installed, you can also test on screen using an on-screen emulator. This can be very slow because the emulator is building a fully featured virtual Android device on top of your current operating system.

Adding On

The Chuck Norris joke generator API allows you to send a parameterized query and insert your name instead of ol' Chuck's in the joke.

You can view the complete documentation for the API here: http://www.icndb.com/api/.

```
▸   ?firstName=
▸   ?lastName=
```

Example 2-11: Adding two parameters to the URL.

1 We're going to take advantage of the API's ability to take parameterized queries and add two parameters to the URL. They are as shown in example 2-11.

So, if we wanted to send a query that would tell us a joke about Ronald Reagan, we'd use the following URL:

http://api.icndb.com/jokes/ random?firstName= Ronald&lastName=Reagan

We'll change up our UI to allow the user to enter a first name and last name and then append that to the URL as a query string before it's sent to the server.

Figure 2-5: The Chuck Norris v2 interface. Notice how jQuery mobile styles the text fields.

```
▸    <div id="container">
▸        <h2>Joke Generator</h2>
▸        <label for="first">First</label>
▸        <input type="text" id="first" />
▸        <label for="last">Last</label>
▸        <input type="text" id="last" />
▸        <button id="btnGetJoke">Get Joke</
    button>
▸        <p>Press the button to retrieve a
    joke.</p>
▸        <div id="joke"></div>
▸    <div> <!--container-->
```

Example 2-12: Altering the code to add the necessary text fields.

```
▸    function getJoke()
▸    {
▸        var url = "http://api.icndb.com/
    jokes/random/?firstName=";
▸        url += document.
    getElementById('first').value;
▸        url += "&lastName=";
▸        url += document.
    getElementById('last').value;
▸        xmlhttp.open('GET', url, false);
▸        xmlhttp.send();
▸    }
```

Example 2-13: Updating the "getJoke ()" function to append the first and last names to the URL.

② We only have to alter two parts of the code to get the desired result. First, the HTML for the user interface (as shown in code example 2-12.)

Here, all we've done is add the necessary fields for the user to enter their first and last name.

③ The Javascript must be able to append the first name and last name to the URL entered as a query string. Only the function shown in example 2-13 must be updated.

You'll notice how the jokes are retrieved from fields and appended to the query string directly.

Note: In production, this is a bad practice; a user can attempt to inject harmful content into the query string via the text fields.

Congratulations! You've completed your week two application. Try not to laugh too hard at the jokes.

For your reference, here's the full code for the Chuck Norris Joke Generator:

The Full Code Listing

```html
<!DOCTYPE html>
<html>
  <head>
    <meta charset="utf-8" />
    <meta name="format-detection" content="telephone=no" />
    <!-- WARNING: for iOS 7, remove the width=device-width and height=device-height
    attributes. See https://issues.apache.org/jira/browse/CB-4323 -->
    <meta name="viewport" content="user-scalable=no, initial-scale=1, maximum-
    scale=1, minimum-scale=1, width=device-width, height=device-height, target-
    densitydpi=device-dpi" />
    <script type="text/javascript" src="phonegap.js"></script>
    <link rel="stylesheet" href="http://code.jquery.com/mobile/1.3.2/jquery.mobile-
    1.3.2.min.css" />
    <script src="http://code.jquery.com/jquery-1.9.1.min.js"></script>
    <script src="http://code.jquery.com/mobile/1.3.2/jquery.mobile-1.3.2.min.js"></
    script>
    <style>
      #container
      {
        margin: 6px;
      }
    </style>
    <script>
    var xmlhttp;

    window.onload=function()
    {
      document.addEventListener("deviceready", init, false);
      //init();
    }
```

```
function init()
    {
       document.getElementById('btnGetJoke').addEventListener('click', getJoke,
false);
       xmlhttp = new XMLHttpRequest();
       xmlhttp.onreadystatechange = receiveJoke;
    }

    function getJoke()
    {
      xmlhttp.open('GET', 'http://api.icndb.com/jokes/random/', false);
      xmlhttp.send();
    }

    function receiveJoke()
    {
      if(xmlhttp.readyState==4 && xmlhttp.status==200)
      {
        var json = jQuery.parseJSON(xmlhttp.responseText);
        console.log(json);
        document.getElementById('joke').innerHTML = json.value.joke;
      }
    }

    </script>
    <title>Chuck Norris Joke Generator</title>
  </head>
  <body>
    <div id="container">
    <h2>Chuck Norris Joke Generator</h2>
    <button id="btnGetJoke">Get Joke</button>
    <p>Press the button to retrieve a Chuck Norris joke.</p>
    <div id="joke"></div>
  </body>
</html>
```

Example 2-14: The completed code for the Chuck Norris Joke Generator.

And version 2, adding the parameterized query:

The Full Code Listing 2

```html
<!DOCTYPE html>
<html>
  <head>
    <meta charset="utf-8" />
    <meta name="format-detection" content="telephone=no" />
    <!-- WARNING: for iOS 7, remove the width=device-width and height=device-height
attributes. See https://issues.apache.org/jira/browse/CB-4323 -->
    <meta name="viewport" content="user-scalable=no, initial-scale=1, maximum-
scale=1, minimum-scale=1, width=device-width, height=device-height, target-
densitydpi=device-dpi" />
    <script type="text/javascript" src="phonegap.js"></script>
    <link rel="stylesheet" href="http://code.jquery.com/mobile/1.3.2/jquery.mobile-
1.3.2.min.css" />
    <script src="http://code.jquery.com/jquery-1.9.1.min.js"></script>
    <script src="http://code.jquery.com/mobile/1.3.2/jquery.mobile-1.3.2.min.js"></
script>
    <style>
      #container
      {
        margin: 6px;
      }
    </style>
    <script>
    var xmlhttp;

    window.onload=function()
    {
      //document.addEventListener("deviceready", init, false);
      init();
    }
function init()
    {
      document.getElementById('btnGetJoke').addEventListener('click', getJoke,
  false);
      xmlhttp = new XMLHttpRequest();
      xmlhttp.onreadystatechange = receiveJoke;
    }
```

```
function getJoke()
{
  var url = "http://api.icndb.com/jokes/random/?firstName=";
  url += document.getElementById('first').value;
  url += "&lastName=";
  url += document.getElementById('last').value;
  xmlhttp.open('GET', url, false);
  xmlhttp.send();
}

function receiveJoke()
{
  if(xmlhttp.readyState==4 && xmlhttp.status==200)
  {
    var json = jQuery.parseJSON(xmlhttp.responseText);
    document.getElementById('joke').innerHTML = json.value.joke;
  }
}

</script>
<title>Chuck Norris Joke Generator</title>
</head>
<body>
  <div id="container">
  <h2>Joke Generator</h2>
  <label for="first">First</label>
  <input type="text" id="first" />
  <label for="last">Last</label>
  <input type="text" id="last" />
  <button id="btnGetJoke">Get Joke</button>
  <p>Press the button to retrieve a joke.</p>
  <div id="joke"></div>
</body>
</html>
```

Example 2-15: Version 2 of the completed Chuck Norris Joke Generator code to include the parameterized query.

Philly Trains

Nothing is more frustrating than standing on a train station platform and not knowing when the next train is coming.

If only there were a mobile app that gave you the time and other relevant information about upcoming trains. If you live in Philadelphia, now there is: Philly Trains.

We're going to build this extremely useful (if you're in Philadelphia) app using our PhoneGap tools and the SEPTA API. You may want to check out the API documentation here: http://www3.septa.org/hackathon/index_old.html.

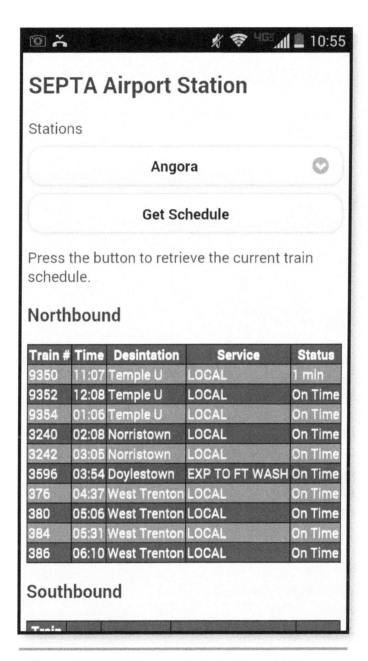

Figure 3-1: Philly Trains app displaying the next trains coming to Angora station.

Getting Ready - Creating the PhoneGap Application

In this initial section of the tutorial we'll create a PhoneGap application and modify the template provided for our own use.

1 With PhoneGap installed, we'll now create the PhoneGap template app. When you create a new PhoneGap application, a template app is installed by PhoneGap. This template is essentially a placeholder and most of it can be removed.
To create the PhoneGap app, make sure your command line is pointed at the location where you want to save the app. I used the desktop. (You can use the **cd** command on the command line to change directories on Mac and PC.) Issue the command shown in example 3-1 to create the PhoneGap template app.

```
phonegap create phillyTrains
```

Example 3-1: Create a new PhoneGap application called "phillyTrains."

```
                        Desktop — bash — 80×24
Last login: Wed Feb  4 08:40:45 on console
Mark-MacBook-Pro:~ marklassoff$ cd Desktop/
Mark-MacBook-Pro:Desktop marklassoff$ phonegap create phillyTrains
Creating a new cordova project with name "Hello World" and id "com.phonegap.hell
oworld" at location "/Users/marklassoff/Desktop/phillyTrains"

Using custom www assets from https://github.com/phonegap/phonegap-app-hello-worl
d/archive/master.tar.gz

Mark-MacBook-Pro:Desktop marklassoff$
```

Figure 3-2: Command line after create template application.

```
<!DOCTYPE html>
<html>
  <head>
    <meta charset="utf-8" />
    <meta name="format-detection"
content="telephone=no" />
    <meta name="msapplication-tap-
highlight" content="no" />
    <!-- WARNING: for iOS 7, remove the
width=device-width and height=device-
height attributes. See https://issues.
apache.org/jira/browse/CB-4323 -->
    <meta name="viewport" content="user-
scalable=no, initial-scale=1, maximum-
scale=1, minimum-scale=1, width=device-
width, height=device-height, target-
densitydpi=device-dpi" />
    <title>Hello World</title>
    <script type="text/javascript"
src="cordova.js"></script>
  </head>
  <body>

  </body>
</html>
```

Example 3-2: The edited template code.

```
<div id="container">
</div> <!-- container -->
```

Example 3-3: Adding a container to the code.

2 The command you issued created a folder called phillyTrains. Open that folder and then the www folder inside it. Inside that folder, delete everything except config.xml and index.html. The files and folders we're deleting are for the template application that we don't need.

3 Open index.html in your text editor. There are references to the template application in the code that we don't need. Edit your code so it appears as shown in example 3-2.

4 The basic template above can be used for any application. Let's add a little HTML and CSS to create a container for our UI. I like using a container because it makes layout easier. We're going to be adding just a few lines of code. Inside the body tag, add the code shown in example 3-3.

5 Next we'll add the CSS to format the container. We'll add some spacing around the margins of the screen to make everything appear more cleanly. Add this code shown in example 3-4 before the closing head tag.

```
<style>
#container
    {
        margin: 8px;
    }
</style>
```

Example 3-4: Styling the container.

Figure 3-3: Code so far in the Brackets editor.

```
<link rel="stylesheet" href="http://code.
jquery.com/mobile/1.3.2/jquery.mobile-
1.3.2.min.css" />
    <script src="http://code.jquery.com/
jquery-1.9.1.min.js"></script>
    <script src="http://code.jquery.com/
mobile/1.3.2/jquery.mobile-1.3.2.min.
js"></script>
```

Example 3-5: Including the jQuery libraries.

6 To add some simple styling, we're going to include the jQuery mobile libraries. By simply adding the libraries, our user interface will appear more mobile-friendly and attractive. If you point your browser to http://jquerymobile.com/download/ you will find the lines of code below. You can paste them directly into your code, above the <style> element.

Making stations.js

Our app has to work for all the stations in the SEPTA system— and there are dozens of them. You obviously don't want to type the station number and station name for each one by hand, due to the strong chance of introducing errors into the code. First, download the available CSV (comma-separated value) file from SEPTA at www3.septa.org/hackathon/Arrivals/station_id_name.csv. The CSV file contains the names and numerical identifiers of all the stations we need. You can open this file in Excel if you wish and examine it.

The CSV format is not optimal for working in Javascript. We need this file to be in JSON format. There are number of good converters on the web, such as the one located at http://www.convertcsv.com/csv-to-json.htm. Paste the CSV content into the textbox and click the "Convert CSV to JSON" button.

Copy the result into a blank text file and save it in the www file in your project under the filename "stations.js".

Using the find and replace feature of your text editor, replace the existing key for the station identifying number with "stationNum" and the existing key for the station name with "stationName" for all the entries.

7 At the beginning of the station.js file, add the variable name and declaration so the very first part of the file appears like example 3-6 shows.

8 Finally, let's switch to the index.html file and add a link to the stations.js Javascript file we just created. Directly below where you added the jQuery links, add the line of code shown in example 3-7.

This will make all of the train stations and station numbers available throughout your program.

```
var stations = [
  {
    "stationNum":90004,
    "stationName":"30th Street Station"
  },
  {
    "stationNum":90314,
    "stationName":"49th St"
  },
  {
    "stationNum":90404,
    "stationName":"Airport Terminal A"
  },
```

Example 3-6: Adding the variable name and declaration.

```
<script src="stations.js"></script>
```

Example 3-7: Adding a link to the *stations.js*.

Creating the User Interface

For this app, we use a fairly simple user interface, styled by jQuery mobile. Here's the HTML you'll need to enter inside the container div you created earlier:

```
<h2>SEPTA Trains</h2>
    <label for="stations">Stations</label>
    <select id="stations">
    </select>
    <button id="btnGetSched">Get Schedule</button>
    <p>Press the button to retrieve the current train schedule.</p>
  <div id="schedule"></div>
```

You'll notice that the select element is empty. We'll dynamically fill in all the station names in option tags in a bit. This will occur when the app is initiated. We also have an empty div id'ed as schedule. This is where we will build the result and display it to the user.

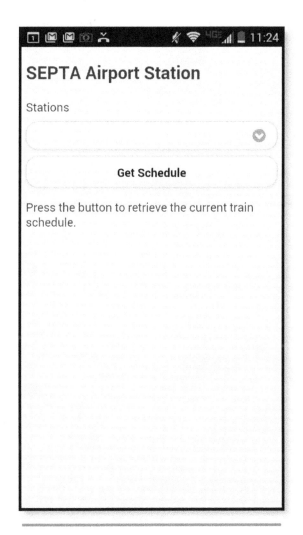

Figure 3-4: The User Interface for our App.

Figure 3-5: The User interface while selecting a station.

Adding the Guts: Javascript to Make it Work

The Javascript for this app has a couple of important jobs. First, it populates the select dropdown from the stations.js file that we created earlier. Next, when the "Get Schedule" button is pushed, it retrieves the schedule as a JSON file from the Septa web service. You can test this in your browser if you'd like. The URL contacted looks like this:

http://www3.septa.org/hackathon/Arrivals/90804/10/

This returns the following JSON code:

```
{
  "Allen Lane Departures: February 4, 2015, 11:34 am":[
    {
      "Northbound":[
        {
          "direction":"N",
          "path":"R8N",
          "train_id":"830",
          "origin":null,
          "destination":"Fox Chase",
          "status":"On Time",
          "service_type":"LOCAL",
          "next_station":null,
          "sched_time":"Feb 4 2015 12:01:00:000PM",
          "depart_time":"Feb 4 2015 12:01:00:000PM",
          "track":"2",
          "track_change":null,
          "platform":" ",
          "platform_change":null
        },
```

```
{
        "direction":"N",
        "path":"R8N",
        "train_id":"832",
        "origin":null,
        "destination":"Fox Chase",
        "status":"On Time",
        "service_type":"LOCAL",
        "next_station":null,
        "sched_time":"Feb 4 2015 12:56:00:000PM",
        "depart_time":"Feb 4 2015 12:56:00:000PM",
        "track":"2",
        "track_change":null,
        "platform":" ",
        "platform_change":null
    },
    {
        "direction":"N",
        "path":"R8N",
        "train_id":"834",
        "origin":null,
        "destination":"Fox Chase",
        "status":"On Time",
        "service_type":"LOCAL",
        "next_station":null,
        "sched_time":"Feb 4 2015 01:55:00:000PM",
        "depart_time":"Feb 4 2015 01:55:00:000PM",
        "track":"2",
        "track_change":null,
        "platform":" ",
        "platform_change":null
    },
    {
        "direction":"N",
        "path":"R8N",
        "train_id":"838",
        "origin":null,
        "destination":"Fox Chase",
        "status":"On Time",
        "service_type":"LOCAL",
```

```
      "next_station":null,
      "sched_time":"Feb 4 2015 02:53:00:000PM",
      "depart_time":"Feb 4 2015 02:53:00:000PM",
      "track":"2",
      "track_change":null,
      "platform":" ",
      "platform_change":null
   },
   {
      "direction":"N",
      "path":"R8\/7N",
      "train_id":"8752",
      "origin":null,
      "destination":"Chestnut H East",
      "status":"On Time",
      "service_type":"LOCAL",
      "next_station":null,
      "sched_time":"Feb 4 2015 03:49:00:000PM",
      "depart_time":"Feb 4 2015 03:49:00:000PM",
      "track":"2",
      "track_change":null,
      "platform":" ",
      "platform_change":null
   },
   {
      "direction":"N",
      "path":"R8N",
      "train_id":"846",
      "origin":null,
      "destination":"Fox Chase",
      "status":"On Time",
      "service_type":"LOCAL",
      "next_station":null,
      "sched_time":"Feb 4 2015 04:37:00:000PM",
      "depart_time":"Feb 4 2015 04:37:00:000PM",
      "track":"2",
      "track_change":null,
      "platform":" ",
      "platform_change":null
   },
```

```
       {
          "direction":"N",
          "path":"R8N",
          "train_id":"850",
          "origin":null,
          "destination":"Fox Chase",
          "status":"On Time",
          "service_type":"LOCAL",
          "next_station":null,
          "sched_time":"Feb 4 2015 05:26:00:000PM",
          "depart_time":"Feb 4 2015 05:26:00:000PM",
          "track":"2",
          "track_change":null,
          "platform":" ",
          "platform_change":null
       },
       {
          "direction":"N",
          "path":"R8N",
          "train_id":"852",
          "origin":null,
          "destination":"Fox Chase",
          "status":"On Time",
          "service_type":"LOCAL",
          "next_station":null,
          "sched_time":"Feb 4 2015 05:57:00:000PM",
          "depart_time":"Feb 4 2015 05:57:00:000PM",
          "track":"2",
          "track_change":null,
          "platform":" ",
          "platform_change":null
       },
       {
          "direction":"N",
          "path":"R8\/7N",
          "train_id":"8764",
          "origin":null,
          "destination":"Chestnut H East",
          "status":"On Time",
          "service_type":"LOCAL",
```

```
          "next_station":null,
          "sched_time":"Feb 4 2015 06:22:00:000PM",
          "depart_time":"Feb 4 2015 06:22:00:000PM",
          "track":"2",
          "track_change":null,
          "platform":" ",
          "platform_change":null
        },
        {
          "direction":"N",
          "path":"R8\/2N",
          "train_id":"8266",
          "origin":null,
          "destination":"Norristown",
          "status":"On Time",
          "service_type":"LOCAL",
          "next_station":null,
          "sched_time":"Feb 4 2015 07:09:00:000PM",
          "depart_time":"Feb 4 2015 07:09:00:000PM",
          "track":"2",
          "track_change":null,
          "platform":" ",
          "platform_change":null
        }
      ]
    },
    {
      "Southbound":[
        {
          "direction":"S",
          "path":"R8S",
          "train_id":"827",
          "origin":"Fox Chase",
          "destination":"Chestnut H West",
          "status":"On Time",
          "service_type":"LOCAL",
          "next_station":"Wayne Jct",
          "sched_time":"Feb 4 2015 12:24:00:000PM",
          "depart_time":"Feb 4 2015 12:24:00:000PM",
          "track":"1",
```

```
        "track_change":null,
        "platform":" ",
        "platform_change":null
    },
    {
        "direction":"S",
        "path":"R8S",
        "train_id":"829",
        "origin":null,
        "destination":"Chestnut H West",
        "status":"On Time",
        "service_type":"LOCAL",
        "next_station":null,
        "sched_time":"Feb 4 2015 01:23:00:000PM",
        "depart_time":"Feb 4 2015 01:23:00:000PM",
        "track":"1",
        "track_change":null,
        "platform":" ",
        "platform_change":null
    },
    {
        "direction":"S",
        "path":"R8S",
        "train_id":"831",
        "origin":null,
        "destination":"Chestnut H West",
        "status":"On Time",
        "service_type":"LOCAL",
        "next_station":null,
        "sched_time":"Feb 4 2015 02:25:00:000PM",
        "depart_time":"Feb 4 2015 02:25:00:000PM",
        "track":"1",
        "track_change":null,
        "platform":" ",
        "platform_change":null
    },
    {
        "direction":"S",
        "path":"R8S",
        "train_id":"833",
```

```
        "origin":null,
        "destination":"Chestnut H West",
        "status":"On Time",
        "service_type":"LOCAL",
        "next_station":null,
        "sched_time":"Feb 4 2015 03:11:00:000PM",
        "depart_time":"Feb 4 2015 03:11:00:000PM",
        "track":"1",
        "track_change":null,
        "platform":" ",
        "platform_change":null
    },
    {
        "direction":"S",
        "path":"R8S",
        "train_id":"835",
        "origin":null,
        "destination":"Chestnut H West",
        "status":"On Time",
        "service_type":"LOCAL",
        "next_station":null,
        "sched_time":"Feb 4 2015 04:08:00:000PM",
        "depart_time":"Feb 4 2015 04:08:00:000PM",
        "track":"1",
        "track_change":null,
        "platform":" ",
        "platform_change":null
    },
    {
        "direction":"S",
        "path":"R8S",
        "train_id":"9837",
        "origin":null,
        "destination":"Chestnut H West",
        "status":"On Time",
        "service_type":"LOCAL",
        "next_station":null,
        "sched_time":"Feb 4 2015 04:46:00:000PM",
        "depart_time":"Feb 4 2015 04:46:00:000PM",
        "track":"1",
```

```
      "track_change":null,
      "platform":" ",
      "platform_change":null
    },
    {
      "direction":"S",
      "path":"R8S",
      "train_id":"839",
      "origin":null,
      "destination":"Chestnut H West",
      "status":"On Time",
      "service_type":"LOCAL",
      "next_station":null,
      "sched_time":"Feb 4 2015 05:11:00:000PM",
      "depart_time":"Feb 4 2015 05:11:00:000PM",
      "track":"1",
      "track_change":null,
      "platform":" ",
      "platform_change":null
    },
    {
      "direction":"S",
      "path":"R8S",
      "train_id":"7841",
      "origin":null,
      "destination":"Chestnut H West",
      "status":"On Time",
      "service_type":"LOCAL",
      "next_station":null,
      "sched_time":"Feb 4 2015 05:46:00:000PM",
      "depart_time":"Feb 4 2015 05:46:00:000PM",
      "track":"1",
      "track_change":null,
      "platform":" ",
      "platform_change":null
    },
    {
      "direction":"S",
      "path":"R7\/8S",
      "train_id":"7843",
```

```
"origin":null,
"destination":"Chestnut H West",
"status":"On Time",
"service_type":"LOCAL",
"next_station":null,
"sched_time":"Feb 4 2015 06:20:00:000PM",
"depart_time":"Feb 4 2015 06:20:00:000PM",
"track":"1",
"track_change":null,
"platform":" ",
"platform_change":null
},
{

"direction":"S",
"path":"R7\/8S",
"train_id":"7845",
"origin":null,
"destination":"Chestnut H West",
"status":"On Time",
"service_type":"LOCAL",
"next_station":null,
"sched_time":"Feb 4 2015 06:44:00:000PM",
"depart_time":"Feb 4 2015 06:44:00:000PM",
"track":"1",
"track_change":null,
"platform":" ",
"platform_change":null
}
]
}
]
}
```

Example 3-8: The full JSON code returned.

(Obviously, since this as a real-time service, the schedule will be different when you contact the URL.) I put this JSON through a formatter, located at http://jsonformatter. curiousconcept.com/, to make it easier for you to read.

As you examine the JSON you can see the information about the next 10 trains traveling in each direction.

Let's enter the Javascript in a <script> tag in the head of our document:

```
var xmlhttp;

    window.onload=function()
    {
       //document.addEventListener("deviceready", init, false);
       init();
    }

    function init()
    {
       document.getElementById('btnGetSched').addEventListener('click', getSchedule,
    false);
       //create station drop down
       for(var i=0; i < stations.length; i++)
       {
          document.getElementById('stations').innerHTML+= "<option value='" +
    stations[i].stationNum + "'>" + stations[i].stationName + "</option>";
       }
    }

    function getSchedule()
    {
       var stationNumber = document.getElementById('stations').value;
       $.ajax({url:"http://www3.septa.org/hackathon/Arrivals/" + stationNumber +
    "/10/",
           success: function(result){
               parseJSON(result);
             }});

       $("#schedule").html("");

    }

    function parseJSON(result)
    {
       var out = "<h3>Northbound</h3>";
       out += "<table class='sced'>";
       out += "<tr class='odd'><th>Train #</th><th>Time</th><th>Destination</
    th><th>Service</th><th>Status</th></tr>"
```

```
        var data = jQuery.parseJSON(result);
        var arr = data[Object.keys(data)];
        var northbound = arr[0].Northbound;
        for(var x=0; x < northbound.length ; x++)
        {
          if((x%2==0))
          {
            out += "<tr class='even'>";
          } else
          {
            out += "<tr class='odd'>";
          }
          var trainID = northbound[x].train_id;
          var destination = northbound[x].destination;
          var service = northbound[x].service_type;
          var status = northbound[x].status;
          var time = northbound[x].depart_time;
          time = time.substring(11,17);
          out += "<td>" + trainID + "</td><td>" + time + "</td><td>" + destination
  + "</td>";
          out += "<td>" + service + "</td><td>" + status + "</td>";
          out += "</tr>"
        }
        out += "</table>";
        document.getElementById('schedule').innerHTML += out;

        var southbound = arr[1].Southbound;
        var out = "<h3>Southbound</h3>";
        out += "<table class='sced'>";
        out += "<tr class='odd'><th>Train #</th><th>Time</th><th>Destination</
  th><th>Service</th><th>Status</th></tr>"
        for(var x=0; x < southbound.length ; x++)
        {

          if((x%2==0))
          {
            out += "<tr class='even'>";
          } else
          {
            out += "<tr class='odd'>";
          }
          var trainID = southbound[x].train_id;
          var destination = southbound[x].destination;
```

```
            var service = southbound[x].service_type;
            var status = southbound[x].status;
            var time = southbound[x].depart_time;
            time = time.substring(11,17);
            out += "<td>" + trainID + "</td><td>" + time + "</td><td>" + destination
  + "</td>";
            out += "<td>" + service + "</td><td>" + status + "</td>";
            out += "</tr>"
        }
      out += "</table>";
      document.getElementById('schedule').innerHTML += out;
    }
```

Example 3-9: Adding the Javascript into the <script> tag.

You will see that much of the coding effort went to parsing the JSON received and formatting it in a table for the user.

Understanding the Code

This initialization process adds the click listener to the button. This runs a function called getSchedule() when the button is clicked. Next, the station dropdown (select element) is created. You'll remember that all the data is loaded into the variable "stations" in the document we created earlier.

The for loop iterates through each key/value pair in the "stations" object. Both the station number and station name are extracted and wrapped in an option element. This option element is then added to the select box.

```
window.onload=function()
    {
        //document.
addEventListener("deviceready", init,
false);
        init();
    }

    function init()
    {
        document.
getElementById('btnGetSched').
addEventListener('click', getSchedule,
false);
        //create station drop down
        for(var i=0; i < stations.length;
i++)
        {
            document.
getElementById('stations').innerHTML+=
"<option value='" + stations[i].stationNum
+ "'>" + stations[i].stationName + "</
option>";
        }
    }
```

Example 3-10: The function that iterates through each key/value pair.

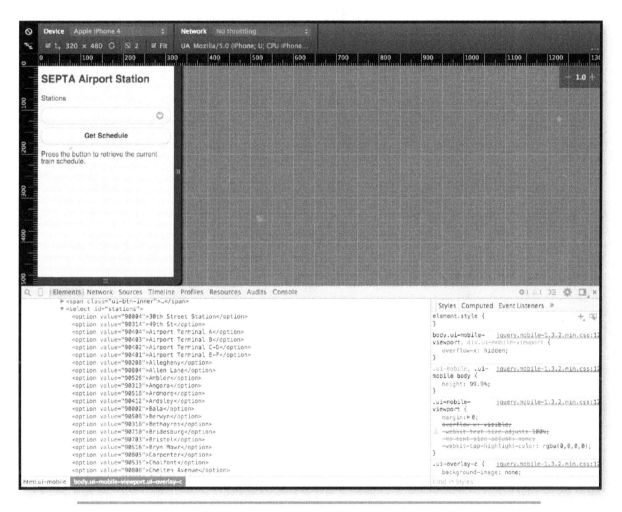

Figure 3-6: Note that in Chrome developer tools you can actually see the option elements nested inside the select element. This view is not a reflection of the HTML code you created, but what is currently stored in the DOM.

When the user depresses the button the getSchedule() function is executed.

```
function getSchedule()
    {
        var stationNumber = document.
getElementById('stations').value;
            $.ajax({url:"http://www3.septa.
org/hackathon/Arrivals/" + stationNumber +
"/10/",
            success: function(result){
                parseJSON(result);
            }});

        $("#schedule").html("");

    }
```

Example 3-11: The "getSchedule ()" function within the code.

This function uses jQuery's $.ajax() function to contact the SEPTA web service URL which is built using the station number from the stations.js file. The JSON result is passed to the parseJSON function, which we'll review next. Finally, the HTML inside the existing schedule div is cleared, in case there was content from a previous lookup still present.

The final function is the most complex one. Here's parseJSON():

```javascript
function parseJSON(result)
    {
        var out = "<h3>Northbound</h3>";
        out += "<table class='sced'>";
        out += "<tr class='odd'><th>Train #</th><th>Time</th><th>Destination</th><th>Service</th><th>Status</th></tr>"
        var data = jQuery.parseJSON(result);
        var arr = data[Object.keys(data)];
        var northbound = arr[0].Northbound;
        for(var x=0; x < northbound.length ; x++)
        {
          if((x%2==0))
          {
            out += "<tr class='even'>";
          } else
          {
            out += "<tr class='odd'>";
          }
            var trainID = northbound[x].train_id;
            var destination = northbound[x].destination;
            var service = northbound[x].service_type;
            var status = northbound[x].status;
            var time = northbound[x].depart_time;
            time = time.substring(11,17);
            out += "<td>" + trainID + "</td><td>" + time + "</td><td>" + destination
    + "</td>";
            out += "<td>" + service + "</td><td>" + status + "</td>";
            out += "</tr>"
        }
        out += "</table>";
        document.getElementById('schedule').innerHTML += out;

        var southbound = arr[1].Southbound;
        var out = "<h3>Southbound</h3>";
        out += "<table class='sced'>";
        out += "<tr class='odd'><th>Train #</th><th>Time</th><th>Destination</th><th>Service</th><th>Status</th></tr>"
        for(var x=0; x < southbound.length ; x++)
```

```
        {

            if((x%2==0))
            {
               out += "<tr class='even'>";
            } else
            {
               out += "<tr class='odd'>";
            }
            var trainID = southbound[x].train_id;
            var destination = southbound[x].destination;
            var service = southbound[x].service_type;
            var status = southbound[x].status;
            var time = southbound[x].depart_time;
            time = time.substring(11,17);
            out += "<td>" + trainID + "</td><td>" + time + "</td><td>" + destination
     + "</td>";
            out += "<td>" + service + "</td><td>" + status + "</td>";
            out += "</tr>"
        }
        out += "</table>";
        document.getElementById('schedule').innerHTML += out;
    }
```

Figure 3-7: The final function: "parseJSON()."

While a bit overwhelming at first, this code breaks down both the southbound and northbound parts of the schedule separately. There is some repeated code here.

Note: Repeated code is generally considered a no-no from a software engineering perspective, however, I choose to repeat code here to make it clearer how the parsing worked.

```
var data = jQuery.parseJSON(result);
var arr = data[Object.keys(data)];
var northbound = arr[0].Northbound;
```

Example 3-12: These lines of code prepare the JSON object for parsing.

First, the northbound schedule is created and a table is created for output inside the out variable.

The code shown in example 3-12 prepare the JSON object for parsing.

We're obtaining just the northbound trains and preparing to loop through them and extract the data. You'll notice in the loop that comes next, we obtain the train id, destination and several other pieces of key information from the JSON. All of this information is stored in local variables. The time comes from the JSON in a format that is not very readable, so a little string manipulation is used to extract the information needed.

Each individual train entry in the JSON is output as an individual table row and then appended to the table itself.

This process is then repeated for the southbound trains.

Testing on a Device

Assuming your device is connected to your computer via USB cable and correctly provisioned (iOS only), you should be able to actually test on your device itself.

If you were testing on an Android device, you should be able to navigate to your project folder using the command line. Once pointed at the project folder, issue the following command:

```
phonegap build android
```

Or, to build on iOS:

```
phonegap build ios
```

If you have the Android SDK installed, you can also test on screen using an on-screen emulator. This can be very slow because the emulator is building a fully featured virtual Android device on top of your current operating system.

Now you've built an app with some real utility. This app isn't all that different than many transit apps already in the app store. Congratulations!

I've got to run— time to catch my train.

For your reference, here's the full code for Philly Trains:

The Full Code Listing

```html
<!DOCTYPE html>
<html>
  <head>
    <meta charset="utf-8" />
    <meta name="format-detection" content="telephone=no" />
    <!-- WARNING: for iOS 7, remove the width=device-width and height=device-height
    attributes. See https://issues.apache.org/jira/browse/CB-4323 -->
    <meta name="viewport" content="user-scalable=no, initial-scale=1, maximum-
    scale=1, minimum-scale=1, width=device-width, height=device-height, target-
    densitydpi=device-dpi" />
    <script type="text/javascript" src="phonegap.js"></script>
    <link rel="stylesheet" href="http://code.jquery.com/mobile/1.3.2/jquery.mobile-
    1.3.2.min.css" />
    <script src="http://code.jquery.com/jquery-1.9.1.min.js"></script>
    <script src="http://code.jquery.com/mobile/1.3.2/jquery.mobile-1.3.2.min.js"></
    script>
    <script src="stations.js"></script>
    <style>
      #container
      {
        margin: 8px;
      }
      table
      {
        font-size: .85em;
        width: 100%;
      }
      .odd
      {
        background-color: #244fa1;
        color: white;
      }
      .even
      {
        background-color: #f1442a;
        color: white;
      }
```

```
      table, th, td
      {
        border: 1px solid black;
        border-collapse: collapse;
      }
    </style>
    <script>
    var xmlhttp;

    window.onload=function()
    {
      //document.addEventListener("deviceready", init, false);
      init();
    }

    function init()
    {
      document.getElementById('btnGetSched').addEventListener('click', getSchedule,
false);
      //create station drop down
      for(var i=0; i < stations.length; i++)
      {
        document.getElementById('stations').innerHTML+= "<option value='" +
stations[i].stationNum + "'>" + stations[i].stationName + "</option>";
      }
    }

    function getSchedule()
    {
      var stationNumber = document.getElementById('stations').value;
      $.ajax({url:"http://www3.septa.org/hackathon/Arrivals/" + stationNumber +
"/10/",
          success: function(result){
            parseJSON(result);
          }});

      $("#schedule").html("");

    }

    function parseJSON(result)
```

```
      {
          var out = "<h3>Northbound</h3>";
          out += "<table class='sced'>";
          out += "<tr class='odd'><th>Train #</th><th>Time</th><th>Destination</
  th><th>Service</th><th>Status</th></tr>"
          var data = jQuery.parseJSON(result);
          var arr = data[Object.keys(data)];
          var northbound = arr[0].Northbound;
          for(var x=0; x < northbound.length ; x++)
          {
            if((x%2==0))
            {
              out += "<tr class='even'>";
            } else
            {
              out += "<tr class='odd'>";
            }
            var trainID = northbound[x].train_id;
            var destination = northbound[x].destination;
            var service = northbound[x].service_type;
            var status = northbound[x].status;
            var time = northbound[x].depart_time;
            time = time.substring(11.17);
            out += "<td>" + trainID + "</td><td>" + time + "</td><td>" + destination
  + "</td>";
            out += "<td>" + service + "</td><td>" + status + "</td>";
            out += "</tr>"
          }
          out += "</table>";
          document.getElementById('schedule').innerHTML += out;

          var southbound = arr[1].Southbound;
          var out = "<h3>Southbound</h3>";
          out += "<table class='sced'>";
          out += "<tr class='odd'><th>Train #</th><th>Time</th><th>Destination</
  th><th>Service</th><th>Status</th></tr>"
          for(var x=0; x < southbound.length ; x++)
          {

            if((x%2==0))
            {
              out += "<tr class='even'>";
```

```
              } else
              {
                out += "<tr class='odd'>";
              }
              var trainID = southbound[x].train_id;
              var destination = southbound[x].destination;
              var service = southbound[x].service_type;
              var status = southbound[x].status;
              var time = southbound[x].depart_time;
              time = time.substring(11,17);
              out += "<td>" + trainID + "</td><td>" + time + "</td><td>" + destination
  + "</td>";
              out += "<td>" + service + "</td><td>" + status + "</td>";
              out += "</tr>"
          }
          out += "</table>";
          document.getElementById('schedule').innerHTML += out;
      }

      </script>
      <title>SEPTA Airport Station</title>
  </head>
  <body>
      <div id="container">
      <h2>SEPTA Trains</h2>
      <label for="stations">Stations</label>
      <select id="stations">
      </select>
      <button id="btnGetSched">Get Schedule</button>
      <p>Press the button to retrieve the current train schedule.</p>
      <div id="schedule"></div>
  </body>
</html>
```

Example 3-13: The complete code listing for the Philly Train application.

And the stations.js file...

Code Listing: stations.js

```
var stations = [
  {
    "stationNum":90004,
    "stationName":"30th Street
Station"
  },
  {
    "stationNum":90314,
    "stationName":"49th St"
  },
  {
    "stationNum":90404,
    "stationName":"Airport Terminal
A"
  },
  {
    "stationNum":90403,
    "stationName":"Airport Terminal
B"
  },
  {
    "stationNum":90402,
    "stationName":"Airport Terminal
C-D"
  },
  {
    "stationNum":90401,
    "stationName":"Airport Terminal
E-F"
  },
  {
    "stationNum":90208,
    "stationName":"Allegheny"
  },
  {
    "stationNum":90804,
    "stationName":"Allen Lane"
  },
  {
    "stationNum":90526,
    "stationName":"Ambler"
  },
  {
    "stationNum":90313,
    "stationName":"Angora"
  },
  {
    "stationNum":90518,
    "stationName":"Ardmore"
  },
  {
    "stationNum":90412,
    "stationName":"Ardsley"
  },
  {
    "stationNum":90002,
    "stationName":"Bala"
  },
  {
    "stationNum":90508,
    "stationName":"Berwyn"
  },
  {
    "stationNum":90318,
    "stationName":"Bethayres"
  },
  {
    "stationNum":90710,
    "stationName":"Bridesburg"
  },
  {
    "stationNum":90703,
    "stationName":"Bristol"
```

```
        },
        {
         "stationNum":90516,
         "stationName":"Bryn Mawr"
        },
        {
         "stationNum":90805,
         "stationName":"Carpenter"
        },
        {
         "stationNum":90535,
         "stationName":"Chalfont"
        },
        {
         "stationNum":90808,
         "stationName":"Chelten Avenue"
        },
        {
         "stationNum":90813,
         "stationName":"Cheltenham"
        },
        {
         "stationNum":90207,
         "stationName":"Chester TC"
        },
        {
         "stationNum":90720,
         "stationName":"Chestnut Hill East"
        },
        {
         "stationNum":90801,
         "stationName":"Chestnut Hill West"
        },
        {
         "stationNum":90204,
         "stationName":"Claymont"
        },
        {
         "stationNum":90309,
         "stationName":"Clifton-Aldan"
        },
        {
         "stationNum":90533,
         "stationName":"Colmar"
        },
        {
         "stationNum":90225,
         "stationName":"Conshohocken"
        },
        {
         "stationNum":90706,
         "stationName":"Cornwells Heights"
        },
        {
         "stationNum":90414,
         "stationName":"Crestmont"
        },
        {
         "stationNum":90704,
         "stationName":"Croydon"
        },
        {
         "stationNum":90209,
         "stationName":"Crum Lynne"
        },
        {
         "stationNum":90216,
         "stationName":"Curtis Park"
        },
        {
         "stationNum":90001,
         "stationName":"Cynwyd"
        },
        {
         "stationNum":90507,
         "stationName":"Daylesford"
        },
        {
         "stationNum":90217,
         "stationName":"Darby"
        },
        {
```

```
      "stationNum":90537,
      "stationName":"Delaware Valley
   College"
      },
      {
      "stationNum":90509,
      "stationName":"Devon"
      },
      {
      "stationNum":90502,
      "stationName":"Downingtown"
      },
      {
      "stationNum":90538,
      "stationName":"Doylestown"
      },
      {
      "stationNum":90219,
      "stationName":"East Falls"
      },
      {
      "stationNum":90405,
      "stationName":"Eastwick Station"
      },
      {
      "stationNum":90705,
      "stationName":"Eddington"
      },
      {
      "stationNum":90208,
      "stationName":"Eddystone"
      },
      {
      "stationNum":90409,
      "stationName":"Elkins Park"
      },
      {
      "stationNum":90228,
      "stationName":"Elm St"
      },
      {
      "stationNum":90301,
      "stationName":"Elwyn Station"
      },
      {
      "stationNum":90504,
      "stationName":"Exton"
      },
      {
      "stationNum":90407,
      "stationName":"Fern Rock TC"
      },
      {
      "stationNum":90312,
      "stationName":"Fernwood"
      },
      {
      "stationNum":90214,
      "stationName":"Folcroft"
      },
      {
      "stationNum":90320,
      "stationName":"Forest Hills"
      },
      {
      "stationNum":90525,
      "stationName":"Ft Washington"
      },
      {
      "stationNum":90532,
      "stationName":"Fortuna"
      },
      {
      "stationNum":90815,
      "stationName":"Fox Chase"
      },
      {
      "stationNum":90713,
      "stationName":"Germantown"
      },
      {
      "stationNum":90310,
```

```
    "stationName":"Gladstone"
  },
  {
    "stationNum":90213,
    "stationName":"Glenolden"
  },
  {
    "stationNum":90411,
    "stationName":"Glenside"
  },
  {
    "stationNum":90719,
    "stationName":"Gravers"
  },
  {
    "stationNum":90528,
    "stationName":"Gwynedd Valley"
  },
  {
    "stationNum":90416,
    "stationName":"Hatboro"
  },
  {
    "stationNum":90517,
    "stationName":"Haverford"
  },
  {
    "stationNum":90206,
    "stationName":"Highland Ave"
  },
  {
    "stationNum":90802,
    "stationName":"Highland"
  },
  {
    "stationNum":90708,
    "stationName":"Holmesburg Jct"
  },
  {
    "stationNum":90222,
    "stationName":"Ivy Ridge"
  },
  {
    "stationNum":90410,
    "stationName":"Jenkintown-Wyncote"
  },
  {
    "stationNum":90324,
    "stationName":"Langhorne"
  },
  {
    "stationNum":90531,
    "stationName":"Lansdale"
  },
  {
    "stationNum":90311,
    "stationName":"Lansdowne"
  },
  {
    "stationNum":90812,
    "stationName":"Lawndale"
  },
  {
    "stationNum":90702,
    "stationName":"Levittown"
  },
  {
    "stationNum":90534,
    "stationName":"Link Belt"
  },
  {
    "stationNum":90227,
    "stationName":"Main St"
  },
  {
    "stationNum":90505,
    "stationName":"Malvern"
  },
  {
    "stationNum":90221,
    "stationName":"Manayunk East"
  },
```

```
    {
      "stationNum":90205,
      "stationName":"Marcus Hook"
    },
    {
      "stationNum":90006,
      "stationName":"Market East"
    },
    {
      "stationNum":90317,
      "stationName":"Meadowbrook"
    },
    {
      "stationNum":90302,
      "stationName":"Media"
    },
    {
      "stationNum":90408,
      "stationName":"Melrose Park"
    },
    {
      "stationNum":90521,
      "stationName":"Merion"
    },
    {
      "stationNum":90223,
      "stationName":"Miquon"
    },
    {
      "stationNum":90306,
      "stationName":"Morton"
    },
    {
      "stationNum":90303,
      "stationName":"Moylan-Rose Valley"
    },
    {
      "stationNum":90717,
      "stationName":"Mt Airy"
    },
    {
      "stationNum":90520,
      "stationName":"Narberth"
    },
    {
      "stationNum":90323,
      "stationName":"Neshaminy Falls"
    },
    {
      "stationNum":90536,
      "stationName":"New Britain"
    },
    {
      "stationNum":90201,
      "stationName":"Newark"
    },
    {
      "stationNum":90226,
      "stationName":"Norristown TC"
    },
    {
      "stationNum":90008,
      "stationName":"North Broad St"
    },
    {
      "stationNum":90523,
      "stationName":"North Hills"
    },
    {
      "stationNum":90711,
      "stationName":"North Philadelphia"
    },
    {
      "stationNum":90529,
      "stationName":"North Wales"
    },
    {
      "stationNum":90212,
      "stationName":"Norwood"
    },
    {
      "stationNum":90811,
```

```
      "stationName":"Olney"                    },
    },                                          {
    {                                             "stationNum":90210,
      "stationNum":90524,                         "stationName":"Ridley Park"
      "stationName":"Oreland"                   },
    },                                          {
    {                                             "stationNum":90515,
      "stationNum":90522,                         "stationName":"Rosemont"
      "stationName":"Overbrook"                 },
    },                                          {
    {                                             "stationNum":90413,
      "stationNum":90506,                         "stationName":"Roslyn"
      "stationName":"Paoli"                     },
    },                                          {
    {                                             "stationNum":90316,
      "stationNum":90527,                         "stationName":"Rydal"
      "stationName":"Penllyn"                   },
    },                                          {
    {                                             "stationNum":90814,
      "stationNum":90530,                         "stationName":"Ryers"
      "stationName":"Pennbrook"                 },
    },                                          {
    {                                             "stationNum":90307,
      "stationNum":90319,                         "stationName":"Secane"
      "stationName":"Philmont"                  },
    },                                          {
    {                                             "stationNum":90215,
      "stationNum":90308,                         "stationName":"Sharon Hill"
      "stationName":"Primos"                    },
    },                                          {
    {                                             "stationNum":90321,
      "stationNum":90211,                         "stationName":"Somerton"
      "stationName":"Prospect Park"             },
    },                                          {
    {                                             "stationNum":90224,
      "stationNum":90809,                         "stationName":"Spring Mill"
      "stationName":"Queen Lane"                },
    },                                          {
    {                                             "stationNum":90512,
      "stationNum":90513,                         "stationName":"St. Davids"
      "stationName":"Radnor"                    },
```

```
  {
    "stationNum":90803,
    "stationName":"St. Martins"
  },
  {
    "stationNum":90715,
    "stationName":"Stenton"
  },
  {
    "stationNum":90510,
    "stationName":"Strafford"
  },
  {
    "stationNum":90005,
    "stationName":"Suburban Station"
  },
  {
    "stationNum":90305,
    "stationName":"Swarthmore"
  },
  {
    "stationNum":90709,
    "stationName":"Tacony"
  },
  {
    "stationNum":90007,
    "stationName":"Temple U"
  },
  {
    "stationNum":90501,
    "stationName":"Thorndale"
  },
  {
    "stationNum":90707,
    "stationName":"Torresdale"
  },
  {
    "stationNum":90701,
    "stationName":"Trenton"
  },
  {
    "stationNum":90322,
    "stationName":"Trevose"
  },
  {
    "stationNum":90807,
    "stationName":"Tulpehocken"
  },
  {
    "stationNum":90406,
    "stationName":"University City"
  },
  {
    "stationNum":90806,
    "stationName":"Upsal"
  },
  {
    "stationNum":90514,
    "stationName":"Villanova"
  },
  {
    "stationNum":90304,
    "stationName":"Wallingford"
  },
  {
    "stationNum":90417,
    "stationName":"Warminster"
  },
  {
    "stationNum":90714,
    "stationName":"Washington Lane"
  },
  {
    "stationNum":90009,
    "stationName":"Wayne Jct"
  },
  {
    "stationNum":90511,
    "stationName":"Wayne"
  },
  {
    "stationNum":90327,
```

```
      "stationName":"West Trenton"
    },
    {
     "stationNum":90503,
     "stationName":"Whitford"
    },
    {
     "stationNum":90514,
     "stationName":"Willow Grove"
    },
    {
     "stationNum":90203,
     "stationName":"Wilmington"
    },
    {
     "stationNum":90220,
     "stationName":"Wissahickon"
    },
    {
     "stationNum":90712,
     "stationName":"Wister"
    },
    {
     "stationNum":90325,
     "stationName":"Woodbourne"
    },
    {
     "stationNum":90718,
     "stationName":"Wyndmoor"
    },
    {
     "stationNum":90003,
     "stationName":"Wynnefield Avenue"
    },
    {
     "stationNum":90519,
     "stationName":"Wynnewood"
    },
    {
     "stationNum":90326,
     "stationName":"Yardley"
```

```
    }
];
```

Example 3-14: The complete code listing for the "stations.js" file.

Current Weather

Storm Chaser: Weather Man

Local weather forecaster Storm Chaser wants to build an app for his legions of viewers and fans. This app will have one simple task: describe the weather conditions for any ZIP code in the country.

This app will use a webservice that returns XML content. Your app will request the XML using a parameterized query. The XML will then be parsed into a readable response which will be displayed for the user.

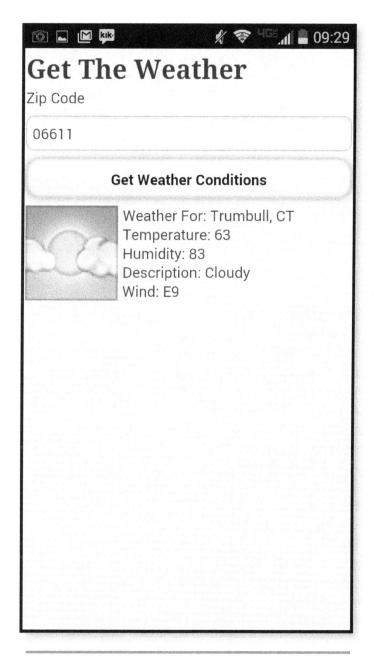

Figure 4-1: Storm's weather app displaying conditions for Trumbull, Connecticut.

Getting Ready - Creating the PhoneGap Application

In this initial section of the tutorial we'll create a PhoneGap application and modify the template provided for our own use.

1 With PhoneGap installed, we'll now create the PhoneGap Template app. When you create a new PhoneGap application, a template app is installed by PhoneGap. This template is essentially a placeholder and most of it can be removed.
To create the PhoneGap app, make sure your command line is pointed at the location where you want to save the app. I used the desktop. (You can use the **cd** command on the command line to change directories on Mac and PC.) Issue the command shown in example 4-1 to create the PhoneGap template app.

```
phonegap create weatherConditions
```

Example 4-1: The command to create the PhoneGap template app.

```
                      Desktop — bash — 80x24
Mark-MacBook-Pro:Desktop marklassoff$ phonegap create weatherConditions
Creating a new cordova project with name "Hello World" and id "com.phonegap.hell
oworld" at location "/Users/marklassoff/Desktop/weatherConditions"
Using custom www assets from https://github.com/phonegap/phonegap-app-hello-worl
d/archive/master.tar.gz

Mark-MacBook-Pro:Desktop marklassoff$ 
```

Figure 4-2: Command line after creating template application creation.

```
<!DOCTYPE html>
<html>
  <head>
    <meta charset="utf-8" />
    <meta name="format-detection"
content="telephone=no" />
    <meta name="msapplication-tap-
highlight" content="no" />
    <!-- WARNING: for iOS 7, remove the
width=device-width and height=device-
height attributes. See https://issues.
apache.org/jira/browse/CB-4323 -->
    <meta name="viewport" content="user-
scalable=no, initial-scale=1, maximum-
scale=1, minimum-scale=1, width=device-
width, height=device-height, target-
densitydpi=device-dpi" />
    <title>Hello World</title>
    <script type="text/javascript"
src="cordova.js"></script>
  </head>
  <body>

  </body>
</html>
```

Example 4-2: The code as it should appear when edited.

```
<div id="container">
</div> <!-- container -->
```

Example 4-3: Adding a container for the UI.

2 The command you issued created a folder called weatherConditions. Open that folder and then the **www** folder inside it. Inside that folder, delete everything except config.xml and index.html. The files and folders we're deleting are for the template application that we don't need.

3 Open index.html in your text editor. There are references to the template application in the code that we don't need. Edit your code so it appears as shown in example 4-2.

4 The template (shown in example 4-2) can be used for any application. Let's add a little HTML and CSS to create a container for our UI. I like using a container because it makes layout easier. We're going to be adding just a few lines of code. Inside the body tag, add the code shown in example 4-3.

5 Next we'll add the CSS to format the container. We'll add some spacing around the margins of the screen to make everything appear more cleanly. Add this code shown in example 4-4 right before the closing head tag.

```
<style>
#container
    {
        margin: 6px;
    }
</style>
```

Example 4-4: Formating the container with some CSS.

```
1  <!DOCTYPE html>
2  <html>
3      <head>
4          <meta charset="utf-8" />
5          <meta name="format-detection" content="telephone=no" />
6          <meta name="msapplication-tap-highlight" content="no" />
7          <!-- WARNING: for iOS 7, remove the width=device-width and height=device-height attributes.
   See https://issues.apache.org/jira/browse/CB-4323 -->
8          <meta name="viewport" content="user-scalable=no, initial-scale=1, maximum-scale=1, minimum-
   scale=1, width=device-width, height=device-height, target-densitydpi=device-dpi" />
9          <title>Hello World</title>
10         <script type="text/javascript" src="cordova.js"></script>
11         <style>
12             #container
13             {
14                 margin: 6px;
15             }
16         </style>
17     </head>
18     <body>
19         <div id="container">
20         </div> <!-- container -->
21     </body>
22 </html>
23
```

Figure 4-3: Code so far in the Brackets editor.

```
    <link rel="stylesheet" href="http://code.
jquery.com/mobile/1.3.2/jquery.mobile-
1.3.2.min.css" />
    <script src="http://code.jquery.com/
jquery-1.9.1.min.js"></script>
    <script src="http://code.jquery.com/
mobile/1.3.2/jquery.mobile-1.3.2.min.
js"></script>
```

Example 4-5: The code to include some jQuery libraries.

6 To add some simple styling, we're going to include the jQuery mobile libraries. By simply adding the libraries, our user interface will appear more mobile-friendly and attractive. If you point your browser to http://jquerymobile.com/download/ you will find the lines of code below. You can paste them directly into your code, above the <style> element.

Creating the User Interface

A quick and easy user interface is used here. Styled by jQuery, the interface includes a text field for the user to enter a ZIP code, a button to retrieve the weather forecast, and an area to display the result. The area where the result is displayed is broken into an image and text area, which displays current conditions.

Here's the HTML:

```
<div id="container">
    <h1>Get The Weather</h1>
    <label for="zip">Zip Code</label>
    <input type="number" id="zip" />
    <button id="btnGetForecast">Get Weather Conditions</button>
    <div id="result">
      <img src="" align="left" id="weatherImage"></img><div id="weatherInfo"></div>
    </div>
</div> <!-- container -->
```

Example 4-6: HTML that will add the user interface elements.

You might want to test the code shown in example 4-6 in your browser and make sure everything looks correct. Use Chrome's Developer Tools mobile emulation to see how your user interface looks on different sized screens.

We also added some additional styling (as shown in example 4-7) to correctly size the image and some of the text.

You may want to experiment with some different images than the ones provided. With bigger images you can set the img width property to render as a percentage, making it appear better on larger screens.

```
h1
    {
        font-size: 1.75em;
        font-family: Georgia;
        font-weight: bold;
    }
#container
    {
        margin: 6px;
    }

img
    {
        width: 100px;
        margin-right: 5px;
    }
```

Example 4-7: Some additional styling to correctly size the image and text.

Adding the Guts: Javascript to Make it Work

This app uses the CDYNE free weather service. This service, unlike the Philly Train service used last week, returns XML (eXtensible Markup Language). XML is a bit harder to work with than JSON. JSON is stored as a native Javascript object, allowing it to be parsed using the traditional dot notation. XML needs to be traversed as a tree structure. The CDYNE weather service documentation is available at http://wiki.cdyne.com/?title=CDYNE_Weather.

This web service accepts parameterized queries, and—in this case—requires one. The ZIP code is provided at the end of the CDYNE URL as a query string. Try pasting this URL into your browser: http://wsf.cdyne.com/WeatherWS/Weather.asmx/GetCityWeatherByZIP?ZIP=06880

```xml
<?xml version="1.0" encoding="utf-8"?>
<WeatherReturn xmlns:xsi="http://
www.w3.org/2001/XMLSchema-instance"
xmlns:xsd="http://www.w3.org/2001/
XMLSchema" xmlns="http://ws.cdyne.com/
WeatherWS/">
  <Success>true</Success>
  <ResponseText>City Found</ResponseText>
  <State>CT</State>
  <City>Westport</City>
  <WeatherStationCity>Bridgeport</
WeatherStationCity>
  <WeatherID>14</WeatherID>
  <Description>Cloudy</Description>
  <Temperature>63</Temperature>
  <RelativeHumidity>83</RelativeHumidity>
  <Wind>E9</Wind>
  <Pressure>29.98F</Pressure>
  <Visibility />
  <WindChill />
  <Remarks />
</WeatherReturn>
```

You should see the current conditions on Westport, Connecticut. (We've had trouble with this server occasionally giving inaccurate information—but, it's FREE. I'll take slightly inaccurate free information over expensive correct information any time!) The information is displayed in XML format rendered by the browser.

Example 4-8 shows an example of the XML returned by the URL above.

Example 4-8: An example of the XML returned by the URL.

Obviously, we can't display this code directly to the user. (We could— but eww!) We need to parse this code and extract the actual information that we want out of it. One of things I really like about XML as opposed to Javascript is that it's self-documenting. I bet most of you can tell me what the temperature was when this XML was produced— even if you've never seen XML code before.

Here's the Javascript code used in this application:

```javascript
var xmlhttp;

window.onload = function()
{
  //document.addEventListener('deviceready', init);
  init();
}

function init()
{
  document.getElementById('btnGetForecast').addEventListener('click',
getData);
}

function getData()
{
  xmlhttp = new XMLHttpRequest();
  xmlhttp.onreadystatechange= processResult;
  var url = "http://wsf.cdyne.com/WeatherWS/Weather.asmx/
GetCityWeatherByZIP?ZIP=";
  url += document.getElementById('zip').value;
  xmlhttp.open("GET", url, false);
  xmlhttp.send();
}

function processResult()
{
  if(xmlhttp.readyState==4 && xmlhttp.status == 200)
  {
```

```
       var theXML = xmlhttp.responseXML.documentElement;
       var city = theXML.getElementsByTagName('City')[0].firstChild.nodeValue;
       var state = theXML.getElementsByTagName('State')[0].firstChild.nodeValue;
       var temperature = theXML.getElementsByTagName('Temperature')[0].
firstChild.nodeValue;
       var relativeHumidity = theXML.getElementsByTagName('RelativeHumidity')
[0].firstChild.nodeValue;
       var description = theXML.getElementsByTagName('Description')[0].
firstChild.nodeValue;
       var wind = theXML.getElementsByTagName('Wind')[0].firstChild.nodeValue;

       var output = "Weather For: ";
       output += city +", " + state;
       output += "<br/>Temperature: " + temperature;
       output += "<br/>Humidity: " + relativeHumidity;
       output += "<br/>Description: " + description;
       output += "<br/>Wind: " + wind;
       var filename = description.toLowerCase();
       filename = filename.replace(/\s+/g, '');
       if (filename=="n/a")
       {
         filename = "na";
       }
       filename += ".gif";
       document.getElementById('weatherImage').src= "icons/" + filename;
       document.getElementById('weatherInfo').innerHTML = output;


   }
 }
```

Example 4-9: The Javascript code this weather application uses.

This Javascript code gets pretty dense, so code carefully.

Understanding the Code

In the very first line of Javascript we declare xmlhttp as a global variable. This will enable us to access the variable anywhere in the code. The standard initialization is used adding a click listener to the button that runs the getData() function when clicked.

The getData() function is where the actions starts.

First, the xmlhttp variable is instantiated as an XMLHttpRequest() object, meaning that it now has all of the properties and functions available to an object of its class. Next, a delegate for the onreadystatechange event is declared. The onreadystatechange event occurs every time the status of server communication changes. We've set processResult() to run when the ready state changes, which will actually happen several times through the life of our program.

```
function getData()
    {
        xmlhttp = new XMLHttpRequest();
        xmlhttp.onreadystatechange=
processResult;
        var url = "http://wsf.
cdyne.com/WeatherWS/Weather.asmx/
GetCityWeatherByZIP?ZIP=";
        url += document.
getElementById('zip').value;
        xmlhttp.open("GET", url, false);
        xmlhttp.send();
    }
```

Example 4-10: The getData() function.

Next, we create the URL by appending the ZIP code to the CDYNE server URL.

Note: You might want to beef up the security here a bit. We're directly appending what the user entered and sending it as a query string. You probably should verify that what you're sending is actually in the form or a ZIP code. Regular Expressions would be perfect for this! (http://www.w3schools.com/jsref/jsref_obj_regexp.asp)

The last two lines of this function, open communication with the server and send the necessary data.

Since we don't know how long it's going to take for the server to respond, nothing much happens now until the ready state changes and the processResult() function is fired. (In reality, the amount of time is often merely milliseconds.)

```
function processResult()
    {
        if(xmlhttp.readyState==4 && xmlhttp.status == 200)
        {

            var theXML = xmlhttp.responseXML.documentElement;
            var city = theXML.getElementsByTagName('City')[0].firstChild.nodeValue;
            var state = theXML.getElementsByTagName('State')[0].firstChild.nodeValue;
            var temperature = theXML.getElementsByTagName('Temperature')[0].
firstChild.nodeValue;
            var relativeHumidity = theXML.getElementsByTagName('RelativeHumidity')
[0].firstChild.nodeValue;
            var description = theXML.getElementsByTagName('Description')[0].
firstChild.nodeValue;
            var wind = theXML.getElementsByTagName('Wind')[0].firstChild.nodeValue;

            var output = "Weather For: ";
            output += city +", " + state;
            output += "<br/>Temperature: " + temperature;
            output += "<br/>Humidity: " + relativeHumidity;
            output += "<br/>Description: " + description;
            output += "<br/>Wind: " + wind;
            var filename = description.toLowerCase();
            filename = filename.replace(/\s+/g, '');
            if (filename=="n/a")
            {
                filename = "na";
            }
            filename += ".gif";
            document.getElementById('weatherImage').src= "icons/" + filename;
            document.getElementById('weatherInfo').innerHTML = output;


        }
    }
```

Example 4-11: The processResult() function.

This is where the bulk of the work takes place.

First we determine if the readyState is four and the status is 200. If **both** of these conditions are true, we know that server communication has successfully completed. The xmlhttp object contains a responseXML object which contains the response from the server. From that object we grab the documentElement, which is our actual XML tree.

This XML is fairly straightforward. There are no repeating nodes, so we don't have to loop through the XML nodes. We do have to DIG, however, to get the information we want out of the XML. For example, to extract the city name from the XML returned:

```
var city = theXML.getElementsByTagName('City')[0].firstChild.nodeValue;
```

From theXML—which contains the entire XML—we use getElementsByTagName() to return an array of the elements with the tag name "City." Since we already know the structure and know there is a single "City" entry, we can safely return the first (zeroth) member of the array. Notice that the method is called get**Elements**ByTagName(). It's going to return an entire element that looks like this:

```
<City>Westport</City>
```

To get at the actual text in the node we need to use the firstChild.nodeValue property. Note that in Javascript the first child of any XML text node is the test in that node.

Using the same technique, we extract the other weather information inside the XML and create output text in the variable output.

We next extract the filename of the image which is done by manipulating the information in the <Description> XML node. The last two lines display the image and the text in the user interface.

Testing on a Device

Assuming your device is connected to your computer via USB cable and correctly provisioned (iOS only), you should be able to actually test on your device itself.

If you were testing on an Android device, you should be able to navigate to your project folder using the command line. Once pointed at the project folder, issue the following command:

```
phonegap build android
```

Or, to build on iOS:

```
phonegap build ios
```

If you have the Android SDK installed, you can also test on screen using an on-screen emulator. This can be very slow because the emulator is building a fully featured virtual Android device on top of your current operating system.

Nice job on this week's app! Hopefully the weather is good where you are.

For your reference, here's the full code for the Weather Conditions app:

The Full Code Listing

```
<!DOCTYPE html>
<html>
  <head>
    <meta charset="utf-8" />
    <meta name="format-detection" content="telephone=no" />
    <meta name="msapplication-tap-highlight" content="no" />
    <!-- WARNING: for iOS 7, remove the width=device-width and height=device-height
attributes. See https://issues.apache.org/jira/browse/CB-4323 -->
    <meta name="viewport" content="user-scalable=no, initial-scale=1, maximum-
scale=1, minimum-scale=1, width=device-width, height=device-height, target-
densitydpi=device-dpi" />
    <link rel="stylesheet" type="text/css" href="http://yui.yahooapis.com/3.17.2/
build/cssreset/cssreset-min.css">
    <script type="text/javascript" src="cordova.js"></script>
    <link rel="stylesheet" href="http://code.jquery.com/mobile/1.3.2/jquery.mobile-
1.3.2.min.css" />
    <script src="http://code.jquery.com/jquery-1.9.1.min.js"></script>
    <script src="http://code.jquery.com/mobile/1.3.2/jquery.mobile-1.3.2.min.js"></
script>
    <style>
      h1
      {
        font-size: 1.75em;
        font-family: Georgia;
        font-weight: bold;
      }
      #container
      {
        margin: 6px;
      }

      img
      {
        width: 100px;
        margin-right: 5px;
      }
    </style>
    <script>
```

```
        var xmlhttp;

        window.onload = function()
        {
          //document.addEventListener('deviceready', init);
          init();
        }

        function init()
        {
          document.getElementById('btnGetForecast').addEventListener('click',
  getData);
        }

        function getData()
        {
          xmlhttp = new XMLHttpRequest();
          xmlhttp.onreadystatechange= processResult;
          var url = "http://wsf.cdyne.com/WeatherWS/Weather.asmx/
  GetCityWeatherByZIP?ZIP=";
          url += document.getElementById('zip').value;
          xmlhttp.open("GET", url, false);
          xmlhttp.send();
        }

        function processResult()
        {
          if(xmlhttp.readyState==4 && xmlhttp.status == 200)
          {

            var theXML = xmlhttp.responseXML.documentElement;
            var city = theXML.getElementsByTagName('City')[0].firstChild.nodeValue;
            var state = theXML.getElementsByTagName('State')[0].firstChild.nodeValue;
            var temperature = theXML.getElementsByTagName('Temperature')[0].
  firstChild.nodeValue;
            var relativeHumidity = theXML.getElementsByTagName('RelativeHumidity')
  [0].firstChild.nodeValue;
            var description = theXML.getElementsByTagName('Description')[0].
  firstChild.nodeValue;
            var wind = theXML.getElementsByTagName('Wind')[0].firstChild.nodeValue;

            var output = "Weather For: ";
```

```
            output += city +", " + state;
            output += "<br/>Temperature: " + temperature;
            output += "<br/>Humidity: " + relativeHumidity;
            output += "<br/>Description: " + description;
            output += "<br/>Wind: " + wind;
            var filename = description.toLowerCase();
            filename = filename.replace(/\s+/g, '');
            if (filename=="n/a")
            {
              filename = "na";
            }
            filename += ".gif";
            document.getElementById('weatherImage').src= "icons/" + filename;
            document.getElementById('weatherInfo').innerHTML = output;


        }
      }


    </script>
    <title>Weather</title>
  </head>
  <body>
    <div id="container">
    <h1>Get The Weather</h1>
    <label for="zip">Zip Code</label>
    <input type="number" id="zip" />
    <button id="btnGetForecast">Get Weather Conditions</button>
    <div id="result">
      <img src="" align="left" id="weatherImage"></img><div id="weatherInfo"></div>
    </div>
    </div> <!-- container -->
  </body>
</html>
```

Example 4-12: The full code listing for this application.

Weather Forecaster

Storm Chaser: Weather Man

Now that local weather forecaster Storm Chaser has made his first app, he wants to build one that is more complex— a weather forecaster.

This app will use the same web service as the previous weather app, but request the more complex forecast XML with the "getCityForecastByZip" operation. The XML is more complex because, unlike the XML for the current weather conditions app, this XML contains multiple repeating nodes. (I've included a sample of the XML at the end of this week's lesson, if you'd like a preview.)

Getting Ready - Creating the PhoneGap Application

In this initial section of the tutorial we'll create a PhoneGap application and modify the template provided for our own use.

1 With PhoneGap installed, we'll now create the PhoneGap Template app. When you create a new PhoneGap application, a template app is installed by PhoneGap. This template is essentially a placeholder and most of it can be removed.
To create the PhoneGap app, make sure your command line is pointed at the location where you want to save the app. I used the desktop. (You can use the **cd** command on the command line to change directories on Mac and PC.) Issue the command shown in example 5-1 to create the PhoneGap template app.

```
phonegap create weatherForecast
```

Example 5-1: The command to create the "whereAmI" template app.

```
Mark-MacBook-Pro:~ marklassoff$ ls
Applications            Downloads              Pictures
Creative Cloud Files    Library                Public
Desktop                 Movies
Documents               Music
Mark-MacBook-Pro:~ marklassoff$ cd Desktop/
Mark-MacBook-Pro:Desktop marklassoff$ phonegap create weatherForecast
Creating a new cordova project with name "Hello World" and id "com.phonegap.hell
oworld" at location "/Users/marklassoff/Desktop/weatherForecast"
Using custom www assets from https://github.com/phonegap/phonegap-app-hello-worl
d/archive/master.tar.g2

Mark-MacBook-Pro:Desktop marklassoff$
```

Figure 5-2: Command line after template application creation.

```
<!DOCTYPE html>
<html>
  <head>
    <meta charset="utf-8" />
    <meta name="format-detection"
content="telephone=no" />
    <meta name="msapplication-tap-
highlight" content="no" />
    <!-- WARNING: for iOS 7, remove the
width=device-width and height=device-
height attributes. See https://issues.
apache.org/jira/browse/CB-4323 -->
    <meta name="viewport" content="user-
scalable=no, initial-scale=1, maximum-
scale=1, minimum-scale=1, width=device-
width, height=device-height, target-
densitydpi=device-dpi" />
    <title>Hello World</title>
    <script type="text/javascript"
src="cordova.js"></script>
  </head>
  <body>

  </body>
</html>
```

Example 5-2: The edited index.html file.

```
<div id="container">
</div> <!-- container -->
```

Example 5-3: Adding a "container" to the code.

2 The command you issued created a folder called weatherForecast. Open that folder and then the **www** folder inside it. Inside that folder, delete everything except config.xml and index.html. The files and folders we're deleting are for the template application that we don't need.

3 Open index.html in your text editor. There are unnecessary references to the template application in the code. Edit your code so it appears as shown in example 5-2.

4 The template shown in example 5-2 can be used for any application. Let's add a little HTML and CSS to create a container for our UI. I like using a container because it makes layout easier. We're going to be adding just a few lines of code. Inside the body tag, add the code shown in example 5-3.

5 Next, we'll add the CSS to format the container. We'll add some spacing around the margins of the screen to make everything appear more cleanly. Add this code right before the closing head tag:

```
<style>
#container
    {
        margin: 6px;
    }
</style>
```

Example 5-4: Formatting the container with some CSS.

```
1  <!DOCTYPE html>
2  <html>
3      <head>
4          <meta charset="utf-8" />
5          <meta name="format-detection" content="telephone=no" />
6          <meta name="msapplication-tap-highlight" content="no" />
7          <!-- WARNING: for iOS 7, remove the width=device-width and height=device-height attributes.
           See https://issues.apache.org/jira/browse/CB-4323 -->
8          <meta name="viewport" content="user-scalable=no, initial-scale=1, maximum-scale=1, minimum-
           scale=1, width=device-width, height=device-height, target-densitydpi=device-dpi" />
9          <title>Hello World</title>
10         <script type="text/javascript" src="cordova.js"></script>
11         <style>
12             #container
13             {
14                 margin: 6px;
15             }
16         </style>
17     </head>
18     <body>
19         <div id="container">
20         </div> <!-- container -->
21     </body>
22  </html>
23
```

Figure 5-3: Code so far in the Brackets editor.

```
   <link rel="stylesheet" href="http://code.
jquery.com/mobile/1.3.2/jquery.mobile-
1.3.2.min.css" />
     <script src="http://code.jquery.com/
jquery-1.9.1.min.js"></script>
     <script src="http://code.jquery.
com/mobile/1.3.2/jquery.mobile-
1.3.2.min.js"></script>
```

Example 5-5: Adding the jQuery mobile libraries.

6 To add some simple styling, we're going to include the jQuery mobile libraries. By simply adding the libraries, our user interface will appear more mobile-friendly and attractive. If you point your browser to http://jquerymobile.com/download/ you will find the lines of code below. You can paste them directly into your code, above the <style> element.

Creating the User Interface

This app uses practically the same HTML as the previous app we developed. We have a title, a space to enter a ZIP code, and a "Get Weather Forecast" button. Nothing fancy here at all! The result <div> remains empty, waiting for the formatted version of the result returned by the server.

Here's the HTML:

```
<div id="container">
    <h1>Get The Weather Forecast</h1>
    <input type="number" id="zip" placeholder="Zip Code"/>
    <button id="btnGetForecast">Get Weather Forecast</button>
    <div id="result">

    </div>
</div> <!-- container -->
```

Example 5-6: The HTML required to create the app's user interface.

As always, once you've got your HTML keyed in for the user interface, check it in the Chrome browser with developers tools. Make sure it looks as you'd expect.

Adding the Guts: Javascript to Make it Work

If you compare the Javascript in this version of the weather app to the previous, you'll note the increased complexity.

We're still querying the CDYNE weather service, but this time, we're using the getCityForecastByZip operation. Like the previous example, this service expects a single parameter in the query that provides the ZIP code. The information returned will include three repeating elements.

The <Forecast> element repeats for each day of the forecast. The CDYNE forecasts are seven days long… so you should expect seven forecast elements included in the XML. Each forecast element looks something like example 5-7.

You'll note that these elements are fairly straightforward, except for the

<ProbabilityOfPrecipitation>

and

<Temperature>

nodes. Both of these are objects and contain child elements them- selves. Due to this structure we'll have to do quite a bit of digging in the XML to get the informa- tion that we need to populate the display.

```
<Forecast>
    <Date>2014-09-21T00:00:00</Date>
    <WeatherID>3</WeatherID>
    <Description>Mostly Cloudy</Description>
    <Temperatures>
      <MorningLow>65</MorningLow>
      <DaytimeHigh>80</DaytimeHigh>
    </Temperatures>
    <ProbabilityOfPrecipiation>
      <Nighttime>20</Nighttime>
      <Daytime>20</Daytime>
    </ProbabilityOfPrecipiation>
</Forecast>
```

Example 5-7: The <Forecast> element.

Here's the Javascript for this app:

```
<script>
    var xmlhttp;

    window.onload = function()
    {
      //document.addEventListener('deviceready', init);
      init();
    }

    function init()
    {
      document.getElementById('btnGetForecast').addEventListener('click',
    getData);
    }

    function getData()
    {
      xmlhttp = new XMLHttpRequest();
      xmlhttp.onreadystatechange= processResult;
      var url = "http://wsf.cdyne.com/WeatherWS/Weather.asmx/
    GetCityForecastByZIP?ZIP=";
      url += document.getElementById('zip').value;
      xmlhttp.open("GET", url, false);
      xmlhttp.send();
    }

    function processResult()
    {
      if(xmlhttp.readyState==4 && xmlhttp.status == 200)
      {

        var theXML = xmlhttp.responseXML.documentElement;
        var city = theXML.getElementsByTagName('City')[0].firstChild.nodeValue;
        var state = theXML.getElementsByTagName('State')[0].firstChild.nodeValue;
        var output = "<h1>Weather For: ";
        output += city +", " + state + "</h1>";
        output += "<ul data-role='listview' id='forecasts'>";
        var forecastResult = theXML.getElementsByTagName('ForecastResult')[0];
        var forecasts = forecastResult.getElementsByTagName('Forecast');
```

```
            //alert(forecasts.length);
            for(var x = 0; x < forecasts.length; x++)
            {

                var date = forecasts[x].getElementsByTagName('Date')[0].firstChild.
    nodeValue;
                var description = forecasts[x].getElementsByTagName('Description')[0].
    firstChild.nodeValue;

                //Image
                 filename = description.replace(/\s+/g, '');
                 if (filename=="n/a")
                 {
                    filename = "na";
                 }
                 filename += ".gif";

                //Get the Temperature from the Temperature Object
                var temp = forecasts[x].getElementsByTagName('Temperatures')[0];
                var morningLow = temp.getElementsByTagName('MorningLow')[0].firstChild.
    nodeValue;
                var daytimeHigh = temp.getElementsByTagName('DaytimeHigh')[0].
    firstChild.nodeValue;

                //Get the Chance of Precip Object
                var probability = forecasts[x].
    getElementsByTagName('ProbabilityOfPrecipiation')[0];
                var nighttimeChance = probability.getElementsByTagName('Nighttime')[0].
    firstChild.nodeValue;
                var daytimeChance = probability.getElementsByTagName('Daytime')[0].
    firstChild.nodeValue;
                output += makeForecastOutput(date, description, temp, morningLow,
    daytimeHigh, daytimeChance, nighttimeChance);

            }
            output += "</ul>";
            document.getElementById('result').innerHTML = output;
            $("#forecasts").listview().listview('refresh');
          }
        }

      function makeForecastOutput(date, description, temp, morningLow, daytimeHigh,
```

```
daytimeChance, nighttimeChance)
    {

        var out= "<li data-role='list-divider'>";
        out += dateFixer(date) + "</li>";
        out += "<li>" + "<img align='left' src='icons/" + filename + "'/>" +
description;
        out += "<br/>Morning Low: " + morningLow + "<br/>Daytime High: " +
daytimeHigh;
        out += "<br/>Chance of precipitation: Daytime " + daytimeChance + "%
Nighttime " + nighttimeChance + "%";
        out += "</li>";
        return out;
    }


    function dateFixer(date)
    {
      var year = date.slice(0,4);
      var day = date.slice(8,10);
      var month = date.slice(5,7);

      return month + "/" + day + "/" + year;
    }

  </script>
```

Example 5-8: The Javascript for this weather forecast app.

Key the code in carefully, as it is very dense in spots.

Note: Even though there are areas where the code is similar to the last script, I would NOT recommend trying to edit the previous code; instead, key in this code from scratch.

Understanding the Code

1 During initialization
we declare a global xmlhttp
variable to facilitate server
communication. We attach a click
listener to the button to begin the
server communication process.

2 Once the user enters a
ZIP code, we'll call the getData()
function which will query the
server and request the forecast
for the ZIP code indicated. The
server will return XML which
we'll parse and display.

3 The function
processResult() does most
of the heavy lifting from this
point on. Once it confirms that
the server response is valid, it
begins breaking down the XML.

```javascript
var xmlhttp;

    window.onload = function()
    {
      //document.
  addEventListener('deviceready', init);
      init();
    }

    function init()
    {
      document.
  getElementById('btnGetForecast').
  addEventListener('click', getData);
    }
```

Example 5-9: The global xmlhttp variable is declared during initialization.

```javascript
function getData()
    {
      xmlhttp = new XMLHttpRequest();
      xmlhttp.onreadystatechange=
  processResult;
      var url = "http://wsf.
  cdyne.com/WeatherWS/Weather.asmx/
  GetCityForecastByZIP?ZIP=";
      url += document.
  getElementById('zip').value;
      xmlhttp.open("GET", url, false);
      xmlhttp.send();
    }
```

Example 5-10: The getData() function.

132 10 Apps in 10 Weeks

```
function processResult()
    {
        if(xmlhttp.readyState==4 && xmlhttp.status == 200)
        {

            var theXML = xmlhttp.responseXML.documentElement;
            var city = theXML.getElementsByTagName('City')[0].firstChild.nodeValue;
            var state = theXML.getElementsByTagName('State')[0].firstChild.nodeValue;
            var output = "<h1>Weather For: ";
            output += city +", " + state + "</h1>";
            output += "<ul data-role='listview' id='forecasts'>";
            var forecastResult = theXML.getElementsByTagName('ForecastResult')[0];
            var forecasts = forecastResult.getElementsByTagName('Forecast');
            //alert(forecasts.length);
            for(var x = 0; x < forecasts.length; x++)
            {

                var date = forecasts[x].getElementsByTagName('Date')[0].firstChild.
    nodeValue;
                var description = forecasts[x].getElementsByTagName('Description')[0].
    firstChild.nodeValue;

                //Image
                 filename = description.replace(/\s+/g, '');
                 if (filename=="n/a")
                 {
                   filename = "na";
                 }
                 filename += ".gif";

                //Get the Temperature from the Temperature Object
                var temp = forecasts[x].getElementsByTagName('Temperatures')[0];
                var morningLow = temp.getElementsByTagName('MorningLow')[0].firstChild.
    nodeValue;
                var daytimeHigh = temp.getElementsByTagName('DaytimeHigh')[0].
    firstChild.nodeValue;

                //Get the Chance of Precip Object
                var probability = forecasts[x].
    getElementsByTagName('ProbabilityOfPrecipiation')[0];
                var nighttimeChance = probability.getElementsByTagName('Nighttime')[0].
```

```
        firstChild.nodeValue;
                var daytimeChance = probability.getElementsByTagName('Daytime')[0].
        firstChild.nodeValue;
                    output += makeForecastOutput(date, description, temp, morningLow,
        daytimeHigh, daytimeChance, nighttimeChance);


            }
            output += "</ul>";
            document.getElementById('result').innerHTML = output;
            $("#forecasts").listview().listview('refresh');
        }
    }
```

Example 5-11: The processResult() function.

First it extracts the city and state from the XML and creates the initial output and stores it in a variable called (smartly) output. It gets ready to store the output in an HTML unordered list with this line of code shown in example 5-12.

```
    output += "<ul data-role='listview'
        id='forecasts'>";
```

Example 5-12: The initial output is stored in an HTML unordered list.

The data-role attribute and value causes the jQuery ListView styling to be applied to the unordered list. You can review the jQuery mobile documentation for more on ListView styling. (http://demos.jquerymobile.com/1.3.0-rc.1/docs/demos/widgets/listviews/) We'll use the id to update the listView control after we've populated it.

Next we have to dig into the XML and extract the individual <forecast> nodes, which hold the daily forecasts we need (as shown in example 5-13.)

The forecasts variable is now an array that we can loop through. Each day's forecast will be a member of the array. We can loop through like this:

```
var forecastResult = theXML.
getElementsByTagName('ForecastResult')[0];
var forecasts = forecastResult.
getElementsByTagName('Forecast');
```

Example 5-13: The individual <forecast> nodes.

```
for(var x = 0; x < forecasts.length; x++)
        {
                var date = forecasts[x].getElementsByTagName('Date')[0].firstChild.
nodeValue;
                var description = forecasts[x].getElementsByTagName('Description')[0].
firstChild.nodeValue;

                //Image
                 filename = description.replace(/\s+/g, '');
                  if (filename=="n/a")
                  {
                    filename = "na";
                  }
                  filename += ".gif";

                //Get the Temperature from the Temperature Object
                var temp = forecasts[x].getElementsByTagName('Temperatures')[0];
                var morningLow = temp.getElementsByTagName('MorningLow')[0].firstChild.
nodeValue;
                var daytimeHigh = temp.getElementsByTagName('DaytimeHigh')[0].
firstChild.nodeValue;

                //Get the Chance of Precip Object
```

```
               var probability = forecasts[x].
getElementsByTagName('ProbabilityOfPrecipiation')[0];
               var nighttimeChance = probability.getElementsByTagName('Nighttime')[0].
firstChild.nodeValue;
               var daytimeChance = probability.getElementsByTagName('Daytime')[0].
firstChild.nodeValue;
               output += makeForecastOutput(date, description, temp, morningLow,
daytimeHigh, daytimeChance, nighttimeChance);

          }
          output += "</ul>";
          document.getElementById('result').innerHTML = output;
          $("#forecasts").listview().listview('refresh');
        }
```

Example 5-14: Code to loop through the forecasts array.

For each forecast node we get the date and description and set those to local variables. Next, we obtain the filename for the image. We then get the high and low temperatures from the temperature object. You'll remember that getElementsByTagName() returns an array, so we have to obtain the zeroth index. You'll also remember that the first child of any XML node in Javascript is the content in that node. We can extract the text in a node with .firstChild.nodeValue.

We parse the ProbabilityOfPrecipitation object to get the chance of precipitation in the night time and day time. We send all the data that's been extracted to a function called makeForecastOutput() which will return a list item node (<li>) that will be appended to our unordered list (which in turn will be formatted by jQuery mobile).

Once all the output is created we display it with these two lines:

```
   document.getElementById('result').innerHTML = output;
   $("#forecasts").listview().listview('refresh');
```

The final line above simply refreshes the listView so that the jQuery styling can be added to the content.

Testing on a Device

Assuming your device is connected to your computer via USB cable and correctly provisioned (iOS only), you should be able to actually test on your device itself.

If you were testing on an Android device, you should be able to navigate to your project folder using the command line. Once pointed at the project folder, issue the following command:

```
phonegap build android
```

Or, to build on iOS:

```
phonegap build ios
```

If you have the Android SDK installed, you can also test on screen using an on-screen emulator. This can be very slow because the emulator is building a fully featured virtual Android device on top of your current operating system.

Great job on this week's project! I hope you found it to be significantly more challenging than the previous week.

For your reference, here's the full code for the Weather Forecast app:

The Full Code Listing

```html
<!DOCTYPE html>
<html>
  <head>
    <meta charset="utf-8" />
    <meta name="format-detection" content="telephone=no" />
    <meta name="msapplication-tap-highlight" content="no" />
    <!-- WARNING: for iOS 7, remove the width=device-width and height=device-height
    attributes. See https://issues.apache.org/jira/browse/CB-4323 -->
    <meta name="viewport" content="user-scalable=no, initial-scale=1, maximum-
    scale=1, minimum-scale=1, width=device-width, height=device-height, target-
    densitydpi=device-dpi" />
    <link rel="stylesheet" type="text/css" href="http://yui.yahooapis.com/3.17.2/
    build/cssreset/cssreset-min.css">
    <script type="text/javascript" src="cordova.js"></script>
    <link rel="stylesheet" href="http://code.jquery.com/mobile/1.3.2/jquery.mobile-
    1.3.2.min.css" />
    <script src="http://code.jquery.com/jquery-1.9.1.min.js"></script>
    <script src="http://code.jquery.com/mobile/1.3.2/jquery.mobile-1.3.2.min.js"></
    script>
    <style>
      h1
      {
        font-size: 1.75em;
        font-family: Georgia;
        font-weight: bold;
      }
      #container
      {
        margin: 6px;
      }

      img
      {
        width: 100px;
        margin-right: 5px;
      }
```

```
        </style>
        <script>
          var xmlhttp;

          window.onload = function()
          {
            //document.addEventListener('deviceready', init);
            init();
          }

          function init()
          {
            document.getElementById('btnGetForecast').addEventListener('click',
      getData);
          }

          function getData()
          {
            xmlhttp = new XMLHttpRequest();
            xmlhttp.onreadystatechange= processResult;
            var url = "http://wsf.cdyne.com/WeatherWS/Weather.asmx/
      GetCityForecastByZIP?ZIP=";
            url += document.getElementById('zip').value;
            xmlhttp.open("GET", url, false);
            xmlhttp.send();
          }

          function processResult()
          {
            if(xmlhttp.readyState==4 && xmlhttp.status == 200)
            {

              var theXML = xmlhttp.responseXML.documentElement;
              var city = theXML.getElementsByTagName('City')[0].firstChild.nodeValue;
              var state = theXML.getElementsByTagName('State')[0].firstChild.nodeValue;
              var output = "<h1>Weather For: ";
              output += city +", " + state + "</h1>";
              output += "<ul data-role='listview' id='forecasts'>";
              var forecastResult = theXML.getElementsByTagName('ForecastResult')[0];
              var forecasts = forecastResult.getElementsByTagName('Forecast');
```

```
            //alert(forecasts.length);
            for(var x = 0; x < forecasts.length; x++)
            {

                var date = forecasts[x].getElementsByTagName('Date')[0].firstChild.
    nodeValue;
                var description = forecasts[x].getElementsByTagName('Description')[0].
    firstChild.nodeValue;

                //Image
                 filename = description.replace(/\s+/g, '');
                 if (filename=="n/a")
                 {
                    filename = "na";
                 }
                 filename += ".gif";

                //Get the Temperature from the Temperature Object
                var temp = forecasts[x].getElementsByTagName('Temperatures')[0];
                var morningLow = temp.getElementsByTagName('MorningLow')[0].firstChild.
    nodeValue;
                var daytimeHigh = temp.getElementsByTagName('DaytimeHigh')[0].
    firstChild.nodeValue;

                //Get the Chance of Precip Object
                var probability = forecasts[x].
    getElementsByTagName('ProbabilityOfPrecipiation')[0];
                var nighttimeChance = probability.getElementsByTagName('Nighttime')[0].
    firstChild.nodeValue;
                var daytimeChance = probability.getElementsByTagName('Daytime')[0].
    firstChild.nodeValue;
                output += makeForecastOutput(date, description, temp, morningLow,
    daytimeHigh, daytimeChance, nighttimeChance);

            }
            output += "</ul>";
            document.getElementById('result').innerHTML = output;
            $("#forecasts").listview().listview('refresh');
          }
        }

    function makeForecastOutput(date, description, temp, morningLow, daytimeHigh,
    daytimeChance, nighttimeChance)
```

```
        {

            var out= "<li data-role='list-divider'>";
            out += dateFixer(date) + "</li>";
            out += "<li>" + "<img align='left' src='icons/" + filename + "'/>" +
    description;
            out += "<br/>Morning Low: " + morningLow + "<br/>Daytime High: " +
    daytimeHigh;
            out += "<br/>Chance of precipitation: Daytime " + daytimeChance + "%
    Nighttime " + nighttimeChance + "%";
            out += "</li>";
            return out;
        }


        function dateFixer(date)
        {
          var year = date.slice(0,4);
          var day = date.slice(8,10);
          var month = date.slice(5,7);

          return month + "/" + day + "/" + year;
        }

    </script>
    <title>Weather</title>
  </head>
  <body>
    <div id="container">
    <h1>Get The Weather Forecast</h1>
    <input type="number" id="zip" placeholder="Zip Code"/>
    <button id="btnGetForecast">Get Weather Forecast</button>
    <div id="result">

    </div>
    </div> <!-- container -->
  </body>
</html>
```

Example 5-15: The full code listing for the weather forecaster app.

Here's some sample XML returned by the service:

```xml
<?xml version="1.0" encoding="utf-8"?>
<ForecastReturn xmlns:xsi="http://www.w3.org/2001/XMLSchema-instance"
xmlns:xsd="http://www.w3.org/2001/XMLSchema" xmlns="http://ws.cdyne.com/
WeatherWS/">
  <Success>true</Success>
  <ResponseText>City Found</ResponseText>
  <State>CT</State>
  <City>Westport</City>
  <WeatherStationCity>Bridgeport</WeatherStationCity>
  <ForecastResult>
   <Forecast>
    <Date>2014-09-20T00:00:00</Date>
    <WeatherID>2</WeatherID>
    <Description>Partly Cloudy</Description>
    <Temperatures>
     <MorningLow>55</MorningLow>
     <DaytimeHigh>72</DaytimeHigh>
    </Temperatures>
    <ProbabilityOfPrecipiation>
     <Nighttime>00</Nighttime>
     <Daytime>10</Daytime>
    </ProbabilityOfPrecipiation>
   </Forecast>
   <Forecast>
    <Date>2014-09-21T00:00:00</Date>
    <WeatherID>3</WeatherID>
    <Description>Mostly Cloudy</Description>
    <Temperatures>
     <MorningLow>65</MorningLow>
     <DaytimeHigh>80</DaytimeHigh>
    </Temperatures>
    <ProbabilityOfPrecipiation>
     <Nighttime>20</Nighttime>
     <Daytime>20</Daytime>
    </ProbabilityOfPrecipiation>
   </Forecast>
   <Forecast>
    <Date>2014-09-22T00:00:00</Date>
    <WeatherID>2</WeatherID>
```

```xml
    <Description>Partly Cloudy</Description>
    <Temperatures>
     <MorningLow>63</MorningLow>
     <DaytimeHigh>69</DaytimeHigh>
    </Temperatures>
    <ProbabilityOfPrecipiation>
     <Nighttime>50</Nighttime>
     <Daytime>10</Daytime>
    </ProbabilityOfPrecipiation>
   </Forecast>
   <Forecast>
    <Date>2014-09-23T00:00:00</Date>
    <WeatherID>4</WeatherID>
    <Description>Sunny</Description>
    <Temperatures>
     <MorningLow>52</MorningLow>
     <DaytimeHigh>70</DaytimeHigh>
    </Temperatures>
    <ProbabilityOfPrecipiation>
     <Nighttime>10</Nighttime>
     <Daytime>10</Daytime>
    </ProbabilityOfPrecipiation>
   </Forecast>
   <Forecast>
    <Date>2014-09-24T00:00:00</Date>
    <WeatherID>4</WeatherID>
    <Desrciption>Sunny</Desrciption>
    <Temperatures>
     <MorningLow>52</MorningLow>
     <DaytimeHigh>67</DaytimeHigh>
    </Temperatures>
    <ProbabilityOfPrecipiation>
     <Nighttime>10</Nighttime>
     <Daytime>10</Daytime>
    </ProbabilityOfPrecipiation>
   </Forecast>
   <Forecast>
    <Date>2014-09-25T00:00:00</Date>
    <WeatherID>4</WeatherID>
    <Description>Sunny</Description>
    <Temperatures>
```

```
      <MorningLow>52</MorningLow>
      <DaytimeHigh>69</DaytimeHigh>
    </Temperatures>
    <ProbabilityOfPrecipiation>
      <Nighttime>10</Nighttime>
      <Daytime>00</Daytime>
    </ProbabilityOfPrecipiation>
  </Forecast>
  <Forecast>
    <Date>2014-09-26T00:00:00</Date>
    <WeatherID>4</WeatherID>
    <Description>Sunny</Description>
    <Temperatures>
      <MorningLow>54</MorningLow>
      <DaytimeHigh>72</DaytimeHigh>
    </Temperatures>
    <ProbabilityOfPrecipiation>
      <Nighttime>00</Nighttime>
      <Daytime>10</Daytime>
    </ProbabilityOfPrecipiation>
  </Forecast>
  </ForecastResult>
</ForecastReturn>
```

Example 5-16: Some sample XML.

Where Am I?

Geolocation

If there has been a "killer feature" for mobile, perhaps, that feature has been geolocation. The integration of location information into mobile apps has led to such famous successes as Yelp and Uber.

This week we're going to make a geolocation app that determines the user's exact latitude and longitude and then displays a Google map of that location. Note that you will need to register for a Google API account— but it's easy and free to do so.

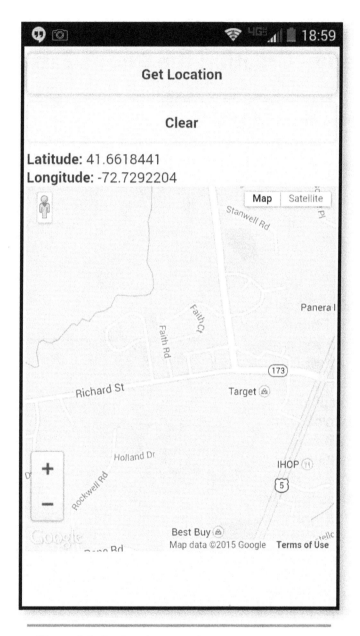

Figure 6-1: Geolocation map displaying latitude, longitude and local map of beautiful Newington, Connecticut.

Getting Ready - Creating the PhoneGap Application

In this initial section of the tutorial we'll create a PhoneGap application and modify the template provided for our own use.

1   With PhoneGap installed, we'll now create the PhoneGap Template app. When you create a new PhoneGap application, a template app is installed by PhoneGap. This template is essentially a placeholder and most of it can be removed.
To create the PhoneGap app, make sure your command line is pointed at the location where you want to save the app. I used the desktop. (You can use the **cd** command on the command line to change directories on Mac and PC.) Issue the command shown in example 6-1 to create the PhoneGap template app.

```
phonegap create whereAmI
```

Example 6-1: The command to create the "whereAmI" template app.

```
                    Desktop — bash — 80×24
Mark-MacBook-Pro:Desktop marklassoff$ phonegap create whereAmI
Creating a new cordova project with name "Hello World" and id "com.phonegap.hell
oworld" at location "/Users/marklassoff/Desktop/whereAmI"
Using custom www assets from https://github.com/phonegap/phonegap-app-hello-worl
d/archive/master.tar.gz

Mark-MacBook-Pro:Desktop marklassoff$
```

Figure 6-2: Command line after template application creation.

```
<!DOCTYPE html>
<html>
  <head>
    <meta charset="utf-8" />
    <meta name="format-detection"
content="telephone=no" />
    <meta name="msapplication-tap-
highlight" content="no" />
    <!-- WARNING: for iOS 7, remove the
width=device-width and height=device-
height attributes. See https://issues.
apache.org/jira/browse/CB-4323 -->
    <meta name="viewport" content="user-
scalable=no, initial-scale=1, maximum-
scale=1, minimum-scale=1, width=device-
width, height=device-height, target-
densitydpi=device-dpi" />
    <title>Hello World</title>
    <script type="text/javascript"
src="cordova.js"></script>
  </head>
  <body>

  </body>
</html>
```

Example 6-2: The edited index.html file.

```
<div id="container">
</div> <!-- container -->
```

Example 6-3: Adding a "container" to the code.

2   The command you issued created a folder called whereAMI. Open that folder and then the **www** folder inside it. Inside that folder, delete everything except config.xml and index.html. The files and folders we're deleting are for the template application that we don't need.

3   Open index.html in your text editor. There are unnecessary references to the template application in the code. Edit your code so it appears as shown in example 6-2.

4   The basic template above can be used for any application. Let's add a little HTML and CSS to create a container for our UI. I like using a container because it makes layout easier. We're going to be adding just a few lines of code. Inside the body tag, add the code shown in example 6-3.

5 Next, we'll add the CSS to format the container. We'll add some spacing around the margins of the screen to make everything appear more cleanly. Add this code right before the closing head tag:

```
<style>
#container
    {
        margin: 6px;
    }
</style>
```

Example 6-4: Formating the container with some CSS.

```
1  <!DOCTYPE html>
2  <html>
3      <head>
4          <meta charset="utf-8" />
5          <meta name="format-detection" content="telephone=no" />
6          <meta name="msapplication-tap-highlight" content="no" />
7          <!-- WARNING: for iOS 7, remove the width=device-width and height=device-height attributes.
   See https://issues.apache.org/jira/browse/CB-4323 -->
8          <meta name="viewport" content="user-scalable=no, initial-scale=1, maximum-scale=1, minimum-
   scale=1, width=device-width, height=device-height, target-densitydpi=device-dpi" />
9          <title>Hello World</title>
10         <script type="text/javascript" src="cordova.js"></script>
11         <style>
12             #container
13             {
14                 margin: 6px;
15             }
16         </style>
17     </head>
18     <body>
19         <div id="container">
20         </div> <!-- container -->
21     </body>
22 </html>
23
```

Figure 6-3: Code so far in the Brackets editor.

```
<link rel="stylesheet" href="http://code.
jquery.com/mobile/1.3.2/jquery.mobile-
1.3.2.min.css" />
    <script src="http://code.jquery.com/
jquery-1.9.1.min.js"></script>
    <script src="http://code.jquery.com/
mobile/1.3.2/jquery.mobile-1.3.2.min.
js"></script>
```

Example 6-5: Adding the jQuery mobile libraries.

6 To add some simple styling, we're going to include the jQuery mobile libraries. By simply adding the libraries, our user interface will appear more mobile-friendly and attractive. If you point your browser to http://jquerymobile.com/download/ you will find the lines of code below. You can paste them directly into your code, above the <style> element.

Creating the User Interface

The user interface for this app could not be easier to create. It consists of just two buttons and blank divs for the latitude and longitude information as well as the map.

Here's the HTML:

```
<div id="container">
    <button id="btnLocation" onclick="getLocation()">Get Location</button>
    <button id="btnClear" onclick="clearScreen()">Clear</button>
    <div id="result"></div>
    <div id="map-canvas"></div>
</div><!-- container-->
```

Example 6-6: The HTML required to create the app's user interface.

You might want to test this in your browser and make sure everything looks correct. Use Chrome's Developer Tools mobile emulation to see how your user interface looks on different sized screens.

We also need some additional CSS code. This code turns off the display of one of the buttons initially and sets a definite height and width for the logical division that will hold the map

```
<style>
    #container {
        margin: 5px;
    }

    #btnLocation  {
        display: none;
    }
    #map-canvas {
        height: 400px;
        width: 100%
    }
    </style>
```

Example 6-7: Some additional CSS to style the buttons.

Hooking up with Google

We'll be pulling in data from the powerful and easy-to-use Google Maps Javascript Api v3. Google offers dozens of APIs that allow registered developers to tap into the power of the Google network. Much of the API content is free for non-commercial usage.

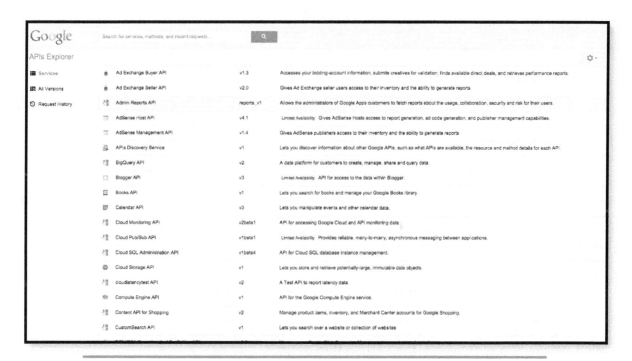

Figure 6-4: Dozens of APIs are part of the Google ecosystem. As a registered developer, you can access many of them within your mobile apps.

If you don't already have a Google account, start by creating one. Google uses a single sign-on paradigm for all of its properties, so you can make one account at https://accounts.google.com/SignUp and access all Google resources.

Once you have your Google sign on, we can move on to the Google Maps API. Note that there are several versions of the API and we're going to be working with Javascript specifically. You can visit the top page of the Google Maps API at https://developers.google.com/maps/documentation/javascript/.

You're going to need your own API key to make your application work. The API key system is used so Google can tell exactly where API requests are coming from and resolve issues or problems. The Google APIs Console located at https://code.google.com/apis/console/ is where you can request your key. Once signed in, go to the services section and click the Google Maps JavaScript API v3 on.

Google Maps Engine API	OFF	Courtesy limit: 10,000 requests/day
Google Maps Geolocation API	OFF	Courtesy limit: 0 requests/day • Pricing
Google Maps JavaScript API v3	ON	Courtesy limit: 25,000 requests/day • Pricing
Google Maps SDK for iOS	OFF	
Google Maps Tracks API	OFF	
Google Mirror API	OFF	Courtesy limit: 1,000 requests/day
Google Picker API	OFF	Courtesy limit: 10,000 requests/day
Google Play Android Developer API	OFF	Courtesy limit: 200,000 requests/day

Figure 6-5: Figure 5: I've turned on the necessary API on the console.

Once you've done this, click the API Access option from the menu and note the API key that's provided. If anyone else ever gets ahold of your key, note that you can also delete and reestablish the key on this page.

Note: It's not that I don't trust you, but in this tutorial I've replaced my API key with XXXXXX in the code listing. Where you see this series of Xs, place the API key that you obtain through Google.

Adding the Guts: Javascript to Make it Work

The first Javascript you'll have to add are the external Javascript libraries for Google Maps. Don't forget to insert the API key you just obtained where I have XXXXXXX.

```
<script src="https://maps.googleapis.com/maps/api/js?key=XXXXXX"></script>
```

This <script> tag should go just below the jQuery inclusion you made when you set up the project.

Next we'll add an additional set of <script> tags and the balance of the Javascript code.

```
<script>
    var options;

    window.onload = function()
    {
      //document.addEventListener('deviceready', init, false);
      init();
    }

    function init()
    {
      document.getElementById('btnLocation').style.display = "block";
      options = { maximumAge: 3000, timeout: 5000, enableHighAccuracy: true };
    }

    function getLocation()
    {
      navigator.geolocation.getCurrentPosition(success, failure, options);
    }

    function success(position)
    {
      var latitude = position.coords.latitude;
      var long = position.coords.longitude;
```

```
              var out = "<strong>Latitude:</strong> " + latitude;
              out += "<br/><strong>Longitude: </strong> " + long;
              document.getElementById('result').innerHTML = out;

              var mapOptions = {
                  center: { lat: latitude, lng: long},
                  zoom: 15
              };
              var map = new google.maps.Map(document.getElementById('map-canvas'),
         mapOptions);

          }

          function failure(message)
          {
            alert("Error:" + message.message);
          }

          function clearScreen()
          {
            document.getElementById('map-canvas').innerHTML = "";
            document.getElementById('map-canvas').style.backgroundColor = "white";
            document.getElementById('result').innerHTML = "";
          }
      </script>
```

Example 6-8: The rest of the Javascript inside some additional <script> tags.

We are taking advantage of both the Javascript geolocation API and the Google Maps API in this code. If you test your application at this point, it should function as advertised.

Understanding the Code

After creating a global variable for geolocation options, we use the standard initialization.

```
window.onload = function()
    {
        //document.
addEventListener('deviceready', init,
false);
        init();
    }

    function init()
    {
        document.
getElementById('btnLocation').style.display
= "block";
        options = { maximumAge: 3000,
timeout: 5000, enableHighAccuracy: true };
    }
```

Example 6-9: The init() function.

```
    function getLocation()
    {
        navigator.geolocation.
getCurrentPosition(success, failure,
options);
    }
```

Example 6-10: The getLocation() function.

1 In the init() function (shown in example 6-9), we turn the location button on by changing the display to "block." We also set our options for geolocation. maximumAge sets how old the oldest geolocation information we'll use can be, and timeout indicates how long we'll wait for new information before throwing an error. By setting the enableHighAccuracy flag to true, we ensure that we are getting the most accurate information possible from the device.

2 When the button is clicked the getLocation() function - shown in example 6-10 - is executed.

You'll notice that the getCurrentPosition() function in example 6-10 has three arguments. The first indicates the callback function to use upon *successfully* receiving geolocation information. The second argument indicates the name of the callback function to use in case of some type of error. The final argument are the options we declared in the previous step.

3 The two callback functions (shown in example 6-11) are next.

The success function is key here. It receives, as an argument, the geolocation information as an object we've called position. Next we extract the latitude and longitude from the object and store those in eponymously named variables.

We use the latitude and longitude to create an output string that we then place in the div IDed as "result". We create a map options object using the latitude and longitude and set the zoom at level 15. This level provides a "neighborhood" level view.

```
function success(position)
    {
        var latitude = position.coords.latitude;
        var long = position.coords.longitude;

        var out = "<strong>Latitude:</strong> " + latitude;
        out += "<br/><strong>Longitude: </strong> " + long;
        document.getElementById('result').innerHTML = out;

        var mapOptions = {
            center: { lat: latitude, lng: long},
            zoom: 15
        };
        var map = new google.maps.Map(document.getElementById('map-canvas'), mapOptions);

    }

    function failure(message)
    {
        alert("Error:" + message.message);
    }
```

Example 6-11: The two callback functions.

```
▸   var map = new google.maps.Map(document.
  getElementById('map-canvas'),
▸     mapOptions);
```

Example 6-12: The line of code that instantiates a new map object and places the visual in the map-canvas element.

```
▸   function clearScreen()
▸       {
▸           document.getElementById('map-
  canvas').innerHTML = "";
▸           document.getElementById('map-
  canvas').style.backgroundColor = "white";
▸           document.getElementById('result').
  innerHTML = "";
▸       }
```

Example 6-13: The clearScreen() function.

4 Finally, the line of code shown in example 6-12 instantiates a new map object and places the visual in the map-canvas element.

Note that this line accesses the Google Maps API that we attached earlier.

5 Our failure() function simply outputs an error message from the error message object passed to the function. Finally, we have a function that clears the results, allowing the user to obtain new geolocation information as desired.

Testing on a Device

Assuming your device is connected to your computer via USB cable and correctly provisioned (iOS only), you should be able to actually test on your device itself.

If you were testing on an Android device, you should be able to navigate to your project folder using the command line. Once pointed at the project folder, issue the following command:

```
phonegap build android
```

Or, to build on iOS:

```
phonegap build ios
```

If you have the Android SDK installed, you can also test on screen using an on-screen emulator. This can be very slow because the emulator is building a fully featured virtual Android device on top of your current operating system.

Congratulations on completing your first geolocation application. Remember: wherever you go, there you are!

For your reference, here's the full code for the "Where Am I?" app:

The Full Code Listing

```html
<!DOCTYPE html>
<!--
  Copyright (c) 2012-2014 Adobe Systems Incorporated. All rights reserved.

  Licensed to the Apache Software Foundation (ASF) under one
  or more contributor license agreements. See the NOTICE file
  distributed with this work for additional information
  regarding copyright ownership. The ASF licenses this file
  to you under the Apache License. Version 2.0 (the
  "License"); you may not use this file except in compliance
  with the License. You may obtain a copy of the License at

  http://www.apache.org/licenses/LICENSE-2.0

  Unless required by applicable law or agreed to in writing,
  software distributed under the License is distributed on an
  "AS IS" BASIS, WITHOUT WARRANTIES OR CONDITIONS OF ANY
   KIND, either express or implied. See the License for the
  specific language governing permissions and limitations
  under the License.
-->
<html>
  <head>
    <meta charset="utf-8" />
    <meta name="format-detection" content="telephone=no" />
    <meta name="msapplication-tap-highlight" content="no" />
    <!-- WARNING: for iOS 7, remove the width=device-width and height=device-height
attributes. See https://issues.apache.org/jira/browse/CB-4323 -->
    <meta name="viewport" content="user-scalable=no, initial-scale=1, maximum-
scale=1, minimum-scale=1, width=device-width, height=device-height, target-
densitydpi=device-dpi" />
     <script type="text/javascript" src="cordova.js"></script>
    <title>Where Am I?</title>
    <link rel="stylesheet" href="http://code.jquery.com/mobile/1.4.5/jquery.mobile-
1.4.5.min.css" />
    <script src="http://code.jquery.com/jquery-1.11.1.min.js"></script>
    <script src="http://code.jquery.com/mobile/1.4.5/jquery.mobile-1.4.5.min.js"></
```

```
script>
    <script src="https://maps.googleapis.com/maps/api/js?key=XXXXXX"></script>
    <script>
      var options;

      window.onload = function()
      {
        //document.addEventListener('deviceready', init, false);
        init();
      }

      function init()
      {
        document.getElementById('btnLocation').style.display = "block";
        options = { maximumAge: 3000, timeout: 5000, enableHighAccuracy: true };
      }

      function getLocation()
      {
        navigator.geolocation.getCurrentPosition(success, failure, options);
      }

      function success(position)
      {
        var latitude = position.coords.latitude;
        var long = position.coords.longitude;

        var out = "<strong>Latitude:</strong> " + latitude;
        out += "<br/><strong>Longitude: </strong> " + long;
        document.getElementById('result').innerHTML = out;

        var mapOptions = {
            center: { lat: latitude, lng: long},
            zoom: 15
        };
        var map = new google.maps.Map(document.getElementById('map-canvas'),
    mapOptions);

      }
```

```
function failure(message)
{
  alert("Error:" + message.message);
}

function clearScreen()
{
  document.getElementById('map-canvas').innerHTML = "";
  document.getElementById('map-canvas').style.backgroundColor = "white";
  document.getElementById('result').innerHTML = "";
}
</script>
<style>
#container {
  margin: 5px;
}

#btnLocation  {
  display: none;
}
#map-canvas {
  height: 400px;
  width: 100%
}
</style>
</head>
<body>
  <div id="container">
    <button id="btnLocation" onclick="getLocation()">Get Location</button>
    <button id="btnClear" onclick="clearScreen()">Clear</button>
    <div id="result"></div>
    <div id="map-canvas"></div>

  </div><!-- container-->

</body>
</html>
```

Example 6-14: The full code listing for the "Where Am I?" app.

I'm Hungry
Google Places API

If you're anything like me, you're ALWAYS hungry.

I built this simple, straightforward app to tell me what the 10 closest, open restaurants are at any given time. The I'm Hungry app contacts the Google Places API, asks for the 10 closest restaurants, and displays their information on the screen.

I'm Hungry

Clear

Elmo's Dockside

48 Hartford Turnpike, Vernon

Google Rating: 4.6

Open Now!

Clam Digger

11 Tolland Turnpike, Manchester

Google Rating:

Open Now!

Subway

53 Hartford Turnpike, Vernon

Figure 7-1: Testing "I'm Hungry" in the browser using Chrome Developer tools. Note that we started the browser using the command line with the following command: **chromium-browser --disable-web-security**. Doing so disabled the cross-site scripting security in the browser.

Getting Ready - Creating the PhoneGap Application

In this initial section of the tutorial we'll create a PhoneGap application and modify the template provided for our own use.

① With PhoneGap installed, we'll now create the PhoneGap Template app. When you create a new PhoneGap application, a template app is installed by PhoneGap. This template is essentially a placeholder and most of it can be removed.
To create the PhoneGap app, make sure your command line is pointed at the location where you want to save the app. I used the desktop. (You can use the **cd** command on the command line to change directories on Mac and PC.) Issue the command shown in example 7-1 to create the PhoneGap template app.

```
phonegap create hungry
```

Example 7-1: The command to create the "hungry" template app.

```
                        Desktop — bash — 80x24
Mark-MacBook-Pro:~ marklassoff$ cd Desktop/
Mark-MacBook-Pro:Desktop marklassoff$ phonegap create hungry
Creating a new cordova project with name "Hello World" and id "com.phonegap.hell
oworld" at location "/Users/marklassoff/Desktop/hungry"

Using custom www assets from https://github.com/phonegap/phonegap-app-hello-worl
d/archive/master.tar.gz

Mark-MacBook-Pro:Desktop marklassoff$
```

Figure 7-2: Command line after template application creation.

```
<!DOCTYPE html>
<html>
  <head>
    <meta charset="utf-8" />
    <meta name="format-detection"
content="telephone=no" />
    <meta name="msapplication-tap-
highlight" content="no" />
    <!-- WARNING: for iOS 7, remove the
width=device-width and height=device-
height attributes. See https://issues.
apache.org/jira/browse/CB-4323 -->
    <meta name="viewport" content="user-
scalable=no, initial-scale=1, maximum-
scale=1, minimum-scale=1, width=device-
width, height=device-height, target-
densitydpi=device-dpi" />
    <title>Hello World</title>
    <script type="text/javascript"
src="cordova.js"></script>
  </head>
  <body>
```

Example 7-2: The edited index.html file.

```
<div id="container">
</div> <!-- container -->
```

Example 7-3: Adding a "container" to the code.

2 The command you issued created a folder called hungry. Open that folder and then the **www** folder inside it. Inside that folder, delete everything except config.xml and index.html. The files and folders we're deleting are for the template application that we don't need.

3 Open index.html in your text editor. There are unnecessary references to the template application in the code. Edit your code so it appears as shown in example 7-2.

4 The template shown in example 7-2 can be used for any application. Let's add a little HTML and CSS to create a container for our UI. I like using a container because it makes layout easier. We're going to be adding just a few lines of code. Inside the body tag, add the code shown in example 7-3.

5 Next, we'll add the CSS to format the container. We'll add some spacing around the margins of the screen to make everything appear more cleanly. Add this code in example 7-4 right before the closing head tag.

```
<style>
#container
    {
        margin: 6px;
    }
</style>
```

Example 7-4: Formatting the container with some CSS.

```
1  <!DOCTYPE html>
2  <html>
3      <head>
4          <meta charset="utf-8" />
5          <meta name="format-detection" content="telephone=no" />
6          <meta name="msapplication-tap-highlight" content="no" />
7          <!-- WARNING: for iOS 7, remove the width=device-width and height=device-height attributes.
   See https://issues.apache.org/jira/browse/CB-4323 -->
8          <meta name="viewport" content="user-scalable=no, initial-scale=1, maximum-scale=1, minimum-
   scale=1, width=device-width, height=device-height, target-densitydpi=device-dpi" />
9          <title>Hello World</title>
10         <script type="text/javascript" src="cordova.js"></script>
11         <style>
12             #container
13             {
14                 margin: 6px;
15             }
16         </style>
17     </head>
18     <body>
19         <div id="container">
20         </div> <!-- container -->
21     </body>
22 </html>
23
```

Figure 7-3: Code so far in the Brackets editor.

```
    <link rel="stylesheet" href="http://code.
jquery.com/mobile/1.3.2/jquery.mobile-
1.3.2.min.css" />
        <script src="http://code.jquery.com/
jquery-1.9.1.min.js"></script>
        <script src="http://code.jquery.com/
mobile/1.3.2/jquery.mobile-1.3.2.min.
js"></script>
```

Example 7-5: Adding the jQuery mobile libraries.

6 To add some simple styling, we're going to include the jQuery mobile libraries. By simply adding the libraries, our user interface will appear more mobile-friendly and attractive. If you point your browser to http://jquerymobile.com/download/ you will find the lines of code below. You can paste them directly into your code, above the <style> element.

Creating the User Interface

Our user interface contains two buttons. The first button causes the device to determine its current location and then retrieve the nearest restaurants from Google. The second button clears the results so you can obtain additional results from another location if desired. There is also a small graphic that is required by users of the Google API at the bottom of the display.

Here's the HTML:

```
<div id="container">
        <button id="btnGetLocation" onclick="getLocation()">I'm Hungry</button>
        <button id="btnClear" onclick="clearScreen()">Clear</button>
        <div id="result"></div>
        <footer>
            <img src="pbg.png" alt="Powered By Google" />
        </footer>
</div><!-- container-->
```

Example 7-6: The HTML required to create the app's user interface.

You might want to test this in your browser and make sure everything looks correct. Use Chrome's Developer Tools mobile emulation to see how your user interface looks on different sized screens.

You should note that both of the buttons have onclick events associated with them. The buttons will call the respective functions when they are clicked.

All of the styling for this app is completed by the jQuery mobile includes in the document <head>.

Hooking up with Google

We'll be pulling in data from the powerful and easy-to-use Google Maps Javascript Api v3. Google offers dozens of APIs that allow registered developers to tap into the power of the Google network. Much of the API content is free for non-commercial usage.

Figure 7-4: Dozens of APIs are part of the Google ecosystem. As a registered developer, you can access many of them within your mobile apps.

If you don't already have a Google account, start by creating one. Google uses a single sign-on paradigm for all of its properties, so you can make one account at https://accounts.google.com/SignUp and access all Google resources.

Once you have your Google sign on, we can move on to the Google Places API.

You're going to need your own API key to make your application work. The API key system is used so Google can tell exactly where API requests are coming from and resolve issues or problems. The Google APIs Console located at https://code.google.com/apis/console/ is where you can request your key. Once signed in, go to the services section and click the Google Places API on.

Figure 7-5: I've turned on the necessary API on the console.

Once you've done this, click the API Access option from the menu and note the API key that's provided. If anyone else ever gets ahold of your key, note that you can also delete and reestablish the key on this page.

Note: In this tutorial I've replaced my API key with XXXXXX in the code listing. Where you see this series of Xs, place the API key that you obtain through Google.

Adding the Guts: Javascript to Make it Work

The Google Places API is a very flexible tool that can return many different types of information. Based on latitude and longitude, the Google Places API can return several different categories of establishments. We'll work with the API via query string. Here's the generic form of the query:

```
https://maps.googleapis.com/maps/api/place/nearbysearch/
xml?key={KEY}&location={latitude},{longitude}&rankby=
{ranking}&keyword={category}
```

In this app, we're obtaining the latitude and longitude using the device's built-in geolocation tools. We'll rank by distance, since we want the 10 closest restaurants. Of course, our keyword category will be "restaurant".

Google will return XML with 10 result nodes, which looks something like this:

```xml
<result>
<name>Jack Demsey's</name>
<vicinity>36 West 33rd Street, New York</vicinity>
<type>bar</type>
<type>restaurant</type>
<type>food</type>
<type>establishment</type>
<geometry>
 <location>
 <lat>40.7483930</lat>
 <lng>-73.9869000</lng>
 </location>
</geometry>
<rating>3.8</rating>
<icon>http://maps.gstatic.com/mapfiles/place_api/icons/bar-71.png</icon>
<reference>CnRvAAAAp7TdpjtFK_GM9jXb1o_S5SI57dDMoEFXNd9DpcdU4yC5pi0xntsIw7Qg55svk5
oKLd5IN0oMr3k1ZIM9RBjaBPsWrUDC6KN9HJy8xrRLmdL8WwndbmlkYoqxxYeEBzY8z-9uzIinLiMOov_
RYXFoSRIQOi4fXuG9VF11YrJTqWtu6RoU5azhVjqiEOcfbMz71zK_JImd8rs</reference>
<id>d77c14862f18849e5ea47a8179e869b89212bfab</id>
<opening_hours>
```

```
<open_now>true</open_now>
</opening_hours>
<photo>
<photo_reference>CnRnAAAAHLTCs9p0MiLrzSK_bDAP_T89K2LcOaoWvY1mrwCjk9Y6-haJbCRZo8oQ
0HIYEtFeWTRjwsYaEkrPkAJyxhKwTeoHFOH9Eryfp3qQl_KFesh9sS6lLqJlq6WWVUNWXVhmejpseHqEWhK
97fNKz5uxmhIQ-mWpc8oF7g36LNkNjC0fURoUFVW8nfKa2TmVvp4WxauRz4QUXzo</photo_reference>
<width>2844</width>
<height>1600</height>
</photo>
<price_level>2</price_level>
<place_id>ChIJW3PAHalZwokRrw41djg_Tik</place_id>
<scope>GOOGLE</scope>
</result>
```

Figure 7-6: An example of the 10 result nodes Google will return.

As you can see, there is much more information in the XML than we need for this little app— but the possibilities for expanding on the app we're building are endless.

Let's take a look at the full Javascript:

```
var xmlhttp;

    window.onload = function()
    {
      //document.addEventListener('deviceready', init, false);
      xmlhttp = new XMLHttpRequest();
      xmlhttp.onreadystatechange = processResult;
    }

    function getLocation()
    {
      var options = {
         enableHighAccuracy: true,
         timeout: 5000,
         maximumAge: 0
      };
      navigator.geolocation.getCurrentPosition(success, failure, options);
```

```
        }

    function success(position)
    {
      var latitude = position.coords.latitude;
      var long = position.coords.longitude;
      var googleURL = "https://maps.googleapis.com/maps/api/place/nearbysearch/
xml?key=XXXXXX&location=";
      googleURL += latitude + "," + long;
      googleURL += "&rankby=distance&keyword=restaurant";
      getRestaurantList(googleURL);
    }

    function getRestaurantList(URL)
    {
      xmlhttp.open("GET", URL, true);
      xmlhttp.send();
    }

    function processResult()
    {
      var out="<ul data-role='listview' data-inset='true' id='restList'>";

      if(xmlhttp.readyState == 4 && xmlhttp.status==200)
      {
        var restaurantXML = $.parseXML(xmlhttp.responseText);
        var xml = $(restaurantXML);
        console.log(xml);
        $(xml).find("result").each(function(){
          var name = $(this).find('name').text();
          var address = $(this).find('vicinity').text();
          var rating = $(this).find('rating').text();
          var open = $(this).find('opening_hours').find('open_now').text();
        // var lat = $(this).find('geometry').find('location').find('lat').
text();
          // var long = $(this).find('geometry').find('location').find('lng').
text();


            //Build output string
            out += "<li data-role='list-divider'><h1>";
            out += name + "</h1></li>";
```

```
            out += "<li>" + address;
            out += "<p>Google Rating: " + rating + "</p>";
            if(open){
               out += "<p class='ul-li-aside'>Open Now!</p>";
            }
            out += "</li>";
         });


      }
      out += "</ul>";
      document.getElementById('result').innerHTML = "<h1>Restaurants Nearby</
h1>";

      document.getElementById('result').innerHTML = out;
      $("#restList").listview().listview('refresh');


   }



   function failure(message)
   {
      alert("Error:" + message.message);
   }

   function clearScreen()
   {
      document.getElementById('result').innerHTML = "";
   }
```

Example 7-7: The full Javascript code for this app.

Don't forget to replace 'XXXXXX' with your API key.

Understanding the Code

1 Our initialization function (shown in example 7-8) instantiates the XMLHttpRequest() object and establishes the callback function as processResult().

2 The getLocation() function (shown in example 7-9) runs when the button on the interface is pressed.

This function first configures the geolocation options object. We want the most current information available and the highest possible accuracy. Once the object is configured, we request the current position from the navigator.geolocation object. There are two callback functions— success() if we obtain a geolocation object from the device, and failure() if we don't and need to report an error to the user.

```
var xmlhttp;

window.onload = function()
{
            //document.
addEventListener('deviceready', init,
false);
        xmlhttp = new XMLHttpRequest();
        xmlhttp.onreadystatechange =
processResult;
    }
```

Example 7-8: The XMLHttpRequest() object.

```
function getLocation()
    {
        var options = {
            enableHighAccuracy: true,
            timeout: 5000,
            maximumAge: 0
        };
        navigator.geolocation.
getCurrentPosition(success, failure,
options);
    }
```

Example 7-9: The getLocation() function.

```
     function success(position)
         {
             var latitude = position.coords.
     latitude;
             var long = position.coords.
     longitude;
             var googleURL = "https://
     maps.googleapis.com/maps/api/place/
     nearbysearch/xml?key=XXXXXX&location=";
             googleURL += latitude + "," +
     long;
             googleURL +=
     "&rankby=distance&keyword=restaurant";
             getRestaurantList(googleURL);
         }
```

Example 7-10: The success() callback function.

```
     function getRestaurantList(URL)
         {
             xmlhttp.open("GET", URL, true);
             xmlhttp.send();
         }
```

Example 7-11: The getRestaurantList() function.

3 The success() callback function (shown in example 7-10) configures the URL to request the local restaurant data from Google.

4 Once the URL is created using the latitude and longitude that have been passed into the function, the URL is passed to getRestaurantList() (shown in example 7-11) which initializes communication with the server.

5 The processResult() function is where the heavy lifting takes place. This function, upon getting a response from the server, parses the XML received, builds an output string in the form of an unordered list, and places the result in the UI for the user to see.

```
function processResult()
    {
        var out="<ul data-role='listview' data-inset='true' id='restList'>";

        if(xmlhttp.readyState == 4 && xmlhttp.status==200)
        {
            var restaurantXML = $.parseXML(xmlhttp.responseText);
            var xml = $(restaurantXML);
            console.log(xml);
            $(xml).find("result").each(function(){
                var name = $(this).find('name').text();
                var address = $(this).find('vicinity').text();
                var rating = $(this).find('rating').text();
                var open = $(this).find('opening_hours').find('open_now').text();
                // var lat = $(this).find('geometry').find('location').find('lat').
    text();
                // var long = $(this).find('geometry').find('location').find('lng').
    text();


                //Build output string
                out += "<li data-role='list-divider'><h1>";
                out += name + "</h1></li>";
                out += "<li>" + address;
                out += "<p>Google Rating: " + rating + "</p>";
                if(open){
                    out += "<p class='ul-li-aside'>Open Now!</p>";
                }
                out += "</li>";
            });


    }
```

```
        out += "</ul>";
        document.getElementById('result').innerHTML = "<h1>Restaurants Nearby</
h1>";

        document.getElementById('result').innerHTML = out;
        $("#restList").listview().listview('refresh');


    }
```

Example 7-12: The processResult() function.

We're using jQuery to more easily parse the XML result in this week's example. Using the jQuery .find() function, we're able to easily locate the elements that we want in each restaurant listing.

> **Note:** We've commented out the code to find the exact latitude and longitude of each restaurant. You may want to use this code to extend this application and add mapping for each restaurant.

Each restaurant is stored in its own <li> element, allowing an attractive output to be built using jQuery mobile. The final line of code refreshes the listview so the dynamic data can be displayed to the user.

Testing on a Device

Assuming your device is connected to your computer via USB cable and correctly provisioned (iOS only), you should be able to actually test on your device itself.

If you were testing on an Android device, you should be able to navigate to your project folder using the command line. Once pointed at the project folder, issue the following command:

```
phonegap build android
```

Or, to build on iOS:

```
phonegap build ios
```

If you have the Android SDK installed, you can also test on screen using an on-screen emulator. This can be very slow because the emulator is building a fully featured virtual Android device on top of your current operating system.

Great job on completing this application. As you can see, we're just scratching the surface of what can be done with geolocation and mobile apps. Let's get something to eat... know a good restaurant nearby?

For your reference, here's the full code for the "I'm Hungry!" app:

The Full Code Listing

```
<!DOCTYPE html>
<!--
   Copyright (c) 2012-2014 Adobe Systems Incorporated. All rights reserved.

   Licensed to the Apache Software Foundation (ASF) under one
   or more contributor license agreements. See the NOTICE file
   distributed with this work for additional information
   regarding copyright ownership. The ASF licenses this file
   to you under the Apache License, Version 2.0 (the
   "License"); you may not use this file except in compliance
   with the License. You may obtain a copy of the License at

   http://www.apache.org/licenses/LICENSE-2.0

   Unless required by applicable law or agreed to in writing,
   software distributed under the License is distributed on an
   "AS IS" BASIS, WITHOUT WARRANTIES OR CONDITIONS OF ANY
    KIND, either express or implied. See the License for the
   specific language governing permissions and limitations
   under the License.
-->
<html>
  <head>
    <meta charset="utf-8" />
    <meta name="format-detection" content="telephone=no" />
    <meta name="msapplication-tap-highlight" content="no" />
    <!-- WARNING: for iOS 7, remove the width=device-width and height=device-height
attributes. See https://issues.apache.org/jira/browse/CB-4323 -->
    <meta name="viewport" content="user-scalable=no, initial-scale=1, maximum-
scale=1, minimum-scale=1, width=device-width, height=device-height, target-
densitydpi=device-dpi" />
      <script type="text/javascript" src="cordova.js"></script>
    <title>I'm Hungry!</title>
    <link rel="stylesheet" href="http://code.jquery.com/mobile/1.4.5/jquery.mobile-
1.4.5.min.css" />
      <script src="http://code.jquery.com/jquery-1.11.1.min.js"></script>
```

```
    <script src="http://code.jquery.com/mobile/1.4.5/jquery.mobile-1.4.5.min.js"></
script>
    <script>
      var xmlhttp;

      window.onload = function()
      {
        //document.addEventListener('deviceready', init, false);
        xmlhttp = new XMLHttpRequest();
        xmlhttp.onreadystatechange = processResult;
      }

      function getLocation()
      {
        var options = {
          enableHighAccuracy: true,
          timeout: 5000,
          maximumAge: 0
        };
        navigator.geolocation.getCurrentPosition(success, failure, options);
      }

      function success(position)
      {
        var latitude = position.coords.latitude;
        var long = position.coords.longitude;
        var googleURL = "https://maps.googleapis.com/maps/api/place/nearbysearch/
xml?key=XXXXXX&location=";
        googleURL += latitude + "," + long;
        googleURL += "&rankby=distance&keyword=restaurant";
        getRestaurantList(googleURL);
      }

      function getRestaurantList(URL)
      {
        xmlhttp.open("GET", URL, true);
        xmlhttp.send();
      }

      function processResult()
      {
        var out="<ul data-role='listview' data-inset='true' id='restList'>";
```

```
          if(xmlhttp.readyState == 4 && xmlhttp.status==200)
          {
            var restaurantXML = $.parseXML(xmlhttp.responseText);
            var xml = $(restaurantXML);
            console.log(xml);
            $(xml).find("result").each(function(){
              var name = $(this).find('name').text();
              var address = $(this).find('vicinity').text();
              var rating = $(this).find('rating').text();
              var open = $(this).find('opening_hours').find('open_now').text();
             // var lat = $(this).find('geometry').find('location').find('lat').
text();
              // var long = $(this).find('geometry').find('location').find('lng').
text();


              //Build output string
              out += "<li data-role='list-divider'><h1>";
              out += name + "</h1></li>";
              out += "<li>" + address;
              out += "<p>Google Rating: " + rating + "</p>";
              if(open){
                out += "<p class='ul-li-aside'>Open Now!</p>";
              }
              out += "</li>";
            });



          }
          out += "</ul>";
          document.getElementById('result').innerHTML = "<h1>Restaurants Nearby</
h1>";
          document.getElementById('result').innerHTML = out;
          $("#restList").listview().listview('refresh');

        }


        function failure(message)
        {
          alert("Error:" + message.message);
```

```
      }

      function clearScreen()
      {
        document.getElementById('result').innerHTML = "";
      }
    </script>
    <style>
    #container {
      margin: 5px;
    }

    #btnLocation  {
      display: none;
    }
    #map-canvas {
      height: 400px;
      width: 100%
    }
    </style>
  </head>
  <body>
    <div id="container">
      <button id="btnGetLocation" onclick="getLocation()">I'm Hungry</button>
      <button id="btnClear" onclick="clearScreen()">Clear</button>
      <div id="result"></div>
      <footer>
        <img src="pbg.png" alt="Powered By Google" />
      </footer>
    </div><!-- container-->

  </body>
</html>
```

Example 7-13: The full code listing for this app.

Scout Compass

Internal Hardware: Compass

Wherever you go, there you are— and this app is designed to help you determine exactly where that is.

We'll dive in to the device hardware this week and use your mobile devices' internal compass to create a Scout-style compass with rotating compass rose.

Figure 8-1: The Scout's Compass App when the device is pointing easterly.

Getting Ready - Creating the PhoneGap Application

In this initial section of the tutorial we'll create a PhoneGap application and modify the template provided for our own use.

1   With PhoneGap installed, we'll now create the PhoneGap Template app. When you create a new PhoneGap application, a template app is installed by PhoneGap. This template is essentially a placeholder and most of it can be removed.
To create the PhoneGap app, make sure your command line is pointed at the location where you want to save the app. I used the desktop. (You can use the **cd** command on the command line to change directories on Mac and PC.) Issue the command shown in example 8-1 to create the PhoneGap template app.

```
phonegap create scoutCompass
```

Example 8-1: The command to create the "scoutCompass" template app.

Figure 8-2: Command line after template application creation.

```
<!DOCTYPE html>
<html>
  <head>
    <meta charset="utf-8" />
    <meta name="format-detection"
content="telephone=no" />
    <meta name="msapplication-tap-
highlight" content="no" />
    <!-- WARNING: for iOS 7, remove the
width=device-width and height=device-
height attributes. See https://issues.
apache.org/jira/browse/CB-4323 -->
    <meta name="viewport" content="user-
scalable=no, initial-scale=1, maximum-
scale=1, minimum-scale=1, width=device-
width, height=device-height, target-
densitydpi=device-dpi" />
    <title>Hello World</title>
    <script type="text/javascript"
src="cordova.js"></script>
  </head>
  <body>
```

Example 8-2: The edited index.html file.

```
<div id="container">
</div> <!-- container -->
```

Example 8-3: Adding a "container" to the code.

2 The command you issued created a folder called scoutCompass. Open that folder and then the **www** folder inside it. Inside that folder, delete everything except config.xml and index.html. The files and folders we're deleting are for the template application that we don't need.

3 Open index.html in your text editor. There are unnecessary references to the template application in the code. Edit your code so it appears as shown in example 8-2.

4 The template shown in example 8-2 can be used for any application. Let's add a little HTML and CSS to create a container for our UI. I like using a container because it makes layout easier. We're going to be adding just a few lines of code. Inside the body tag, add the code shown in example 8-3.

5 Next, we'll add the CSS to format the container. We'll add some spacing around the margins of the screen to make everything appear more cleanly. Add this code in example 7-4 right before the closing head tag.

```
<style>
#container
    {
        margin: 6px;
    }
</style>
```

Example 8-4: Formatting the container with some CSS.

```
1  <!DOCTYPE html>
2  <html>
3      <head>
4          <meta charset="utf-8" />
5          <meta name="format-detection" content="telephone=no" />
6          <meta name="msapplication-tap-highlight" content="no" />
7          <!-- WARNING: for iOS 7, remove the width=device-width and height=device-height attributes.
   See https://issues.apache.org/jira/browse/CB-4323 -->
8          <meta name="viewport" content="user-scalable=no, initial-scale=1, maximum-scale=1, minimum-
   scale=1, width=device-width, height=device-height, target-densitydpi=device-dpi" />
9          <title>Hello World</title>
10         <script type="text/javascript" src="cordova.js"></script>
11         <style>
12             #container
13             {
14                 margin: 6px;
15             }
16         </style>
17     </head>
18     <body>
19         <div id="container">
20         </div> <!-- container -->
21     </body>
22  </html>
23
```

Figure 8-3: Code so far in the Brackets editor.

```
▸    <link rel="stylesheet" href="http://code.
     jquery.com/mobile/1.3.2/jquery.mobile-
     1.3.2.min.css" />
▸       <script src="http://code.jquery.com/
     jquery-1.9.1.min.js"></script>
▸       <script src="http://code.jquery.com/
     mobile/1.3.2/jquery.mobile-1.3.2.min.
     js"></script>
```

Example 8-5: Adding the jQuery mobile libraries.

6 To add some simple styling, we're going to include the jQuery mobile libraries. By simply adding the libraries, our user interface will appear more mobile-friendly and attractive. If you point your browser to http://jquerymobile.com/download/ you will find the lines of code shown in example 8-5. You can paste them directly into your code, above the <style> element.

Adding the Compass Library

Current versions of PhoneGap use a modular architecture. This reduces the overall size and footprint of PhoneGap as unnecessary components and libraries are not included in your app. We do have to explicitly load libraries we'll be needing into our app itself. Open your project folder in the command line and type the following command:

```
▸  cordova plugin add org.apache.cordova.device-orientation
```

Once the command executes, the device-orientation library will be installed into the project. This will give us access to the native libraries (for each specific flavor of mobile device) and the Javascript code that gives us access to the native code. In essence, this will make the compass work.

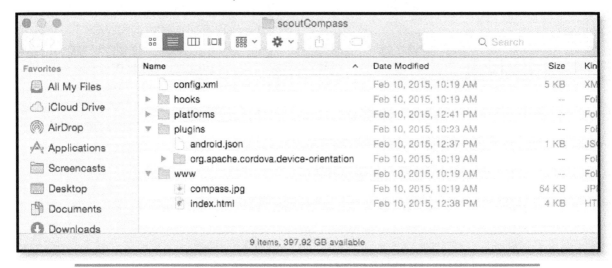

Figure 8-4: The device-orientation library is loaded into the plugins folder as a Java package and JSON support file.

Creating the User Interface

There is almost no user interface for this application. The user doesn't interact with the app—the app just provides the required output. In order to display the output we first create a <div> to hold the compass rose graphic. We're going to place the graphic on a canvas element. If you haven't worked with the canvas much before, you'll likely find this new HTML5 structure very useful.

```
<div id="container">
    <div id="compassRose">
        <canvas id="myCanvas"></canvas>
    </div>
    <div id="compassNumerical">12</div>
</div>
```

Example 8-6: Adding some more divs inside the "container."

```
#container
{
    margin: 6px;
}

#compassNumerical{
    text-align: center;
    font-size: 6em;
    font-family: Arial, Verdana, sans-
serif;
    font-weight: bold;
}
#compassRose /*img*/
{
    width: 300px;
    height: 334px;
    margin-left: auto;
    margin-right: auto;
}
```

Example 8-7: Styling the text ouput and image.

The campus is essentially a drawing surface— much like Adobe Flash's stage. It allows us to easily rotate graphical elements which will be necessary in this app. The "compassNumerical" <div> (shown in example 8-6) will hold a numerical output for the compass— a value between 0° and 359°.

We do need to add some CSS code to style the text output and the compass rose image. Add this code shown in example 8-7 inside a style element.

Adding the Guts: Javascript to Make it Work

We use a number of global variables in this script. The compass direction is read several times per second and the direction is output while the compass rose graphic is rotated appropriately.

```
var watch;
    var cnv;
    var cnvWidth = 300;
    var cnvHeight = 334;
    var curDegrees = 0;
    var img;

    window.onload=function()
    {
      document.addEventListener('deviceready', init, true);
      //init();
    }

    function init()
    {
      var options = { frequency: 200 };
      watch = navigator.compass.watchHeading(success, fail, options);
      cnv = document.getElementById('myCanvas').getContext('2d');
      cnv.canvas.width = cnvWidth;
      cnv.canvas.height = cnvHeight;

      img = new Image();
      img.onload = function()
      {
        cnv.drawImage(img, 0, 0);
      }
      img.src = "compass.jpg";
    }

    function success(compass)
    {
      document.getElementById('compassNumerical').innerHTML = Math.round(compass.
```

```
magneticHeading) + "&deg;";

        var degreeMove = curDegrees - compass.magneticHeading;
        curDegrees = compass.magneticHeading;

        cnv.clearRect(0,0,cnvWidth, cnvHeight);
        cnv.translate(cnvWidth/2, cnvHeight/2);
        cnv.rotate(degreeMove*Math.PI/180);
        cnv.translate(-cnvWidth/2, -cnvHeight/2);
        cnv.drawImage(img, 0, 0);
    }

    function fail(error)
    {
        alert("Error: " + error.code);
    }
```

Example 8-8: The Javascript to make the compass app work.

As always, be careful keying in the code, as a single error can break your app!

Understanding the Code

After declaring a number of global variables we have a fairly extensive initialization process.

Once we have our device ready event, the init() function (shown in example 8-9) has a number of important tasks. First we create the options object for the compass. In this case, the options declare that we want a reading from the compass every 200 milliseconds. Next, we set up the compass itself and name our callback functions: success() for successful compass readings and fail() for compass errors.

We set up the canvas and declare its width and height. Finally we dynamically load the compass image and draw it on the canvas surface. We have to be a bit careful as we do this. The next line of code will execute before the file has time to load. If we use draw() image before the image actually loads, nothing will be drawn. To combat this possible "race condition," we attach an onload event to the image object. Only after the image fully loads is the drawImage() function executed.

```
window.onload=function()
    {
        document.
addEventListener('deviceready', init, true);
        //init();
    }

    function init()
    {
        var options = { frequency: 200 };
        watch = navigator.compass.
watchHeading(success, fail, options);
            cnv = document.
getElementById('myCanvas').
getContext('2d');
                cnv.canvas.width = cnvWidth;
                cnv.canvas.height = cnvHeight;

            img = new Image();
            img.onload = function()
            {
                cnv.drawImage(img, 0, 0);
            }
            img.src = "compass.jpg";
    }
```

Example 8-9: The initialization process.

```
    function success(compass)
        {
            document.
getElementById('compassNumerical').
innerHTML = Math.round(compass.
magneticHeading) + "&deg;";

            var degreeMove = curDegrees -
compass.magneticHeading;
            curDegrees = compass.
magneticHeading;

            cnv.clearRect(0,0,cnvWidth,
cnvHeight);
            cnv.translate(cnvWidth/2,
cnvHeight/2);
            cnv.rotate(degreeMove*Math.PI/180);
            cnv.translate(-cnvWidth/2,
-cnvHeight/2);
            cnv.drawImage(img, 0, 0);
        }
```

Example 8-10: The success function.

The success function (shown in example 8-10) is run five times a second, upon receiving a successful compass reading.

First the magnetic heading is output to the "compassNumerical" <div> we created in the user interface. Next the degrees to rotate the canvas is calculated. The compass rose is then rotated and redrawn. To rotate the compass rose appropriately we have to move the registration point with translate(). We need to rotate the canvas from the middle, but draw it from the top left-hand corner.

Testing on a Device

Assuming your device is connected to your computer via USB cable and correctly provisioned (iOS only), you should be able to actually test on your device itself.

If you were testing on an Android device, you should be able to navigate to your project folder using the command line. Once pointed at the project folder, issue the following command:

```
phonegap build android
```

Or, to build on iOS:

```
phonegap build ios
```

If you have the Android SDK installed, you can also test on screen using an on-screen emulator. This can be very slow because the emulator is building a fully featured virtual Android device on top of your current operating system.

Another week, another completed app. Now get lost! (Don't worry, you can use the Scout Compass to find your way back.)

For your reference, here's the full code for the "Scout Compass" app:

The Full Code Listing

```
<!DOCTYPE html>
<!--
    Copyright (c) 2012-2014 Adobe Systems Incorporated. All rights reserved.

    Licensed to the Apache Software Foundation (ASF) under one
    or more contributor license agreements. See the NOTICE file
    distributed with this work for additional information
    regarding copyright ownership. The ASF licenses this file
    to you under the Apache License, Version 2.0 (the
    "License"); you may not use this file except in compliance
    with the License. You may obtain a copy of the License at

    http://www.apache.org/licenses/LICENSE-2.0

    Unless required by applicable law or agreed to in writing,
    software distributed under the License is distributed on an
    "AS IS" BASIS, WITHOUT WARRANTIES OR CONDITIONS OF ANY
     KIND, either express or implied. See the License for the
    specific language governing permissions and limitations
    under the License.
-->
<html>
  <head>
    <meta charset="utf-8" />
    <meta name="format-detection" content="telephone=no" />
    <meta name="msapplication-tap-highlight" content="no" />
    <!-- WARNING: for iOS 7, remove the width=device-width and height=device-height
attributes. See https://issues.apache.org/jira/browse/CB-4323 -->
    <meta name="viewport" content="user-scalable=no, initial-scale=1, maximum-
scale=1, minimum-scale=1, width=device-width, height=device-height, target-
densitydpi=device-dpi" />
    <script type="text/javascript" src="cordova.js"></script>
    <script>
      var watch;
      var cnv;
      var cnvWidth = 300;
      var cnvHeight = 334;
      var curDegrees = 0;
```

```
var img;

window.onload=function()
{
  document.addEventListener('deviceready', init, true);
  //init();
}

function init()
{
  var options = { frequency: 200 };
  watch = navigator.compass.watchHeading(success, fail, options);
  cnv = document.getElementById('myCanvas').getContext('2d');
  cnv.canvas.width = cnvWidth;
  cnv.canvas.height = cnvHeight;

  img = new Image();
  img.onload = function()
  {
    cnv.drawImage(img, 0, 0);
  }
  img.src = "compass.jpg";
}

function success(compass)
{
  document.getElementById('compassNumerical').innerHTML = Math.round(compass.
magneticHeading) + "&deg;";

  var degreeMove = curDegrees - compass.magneticHeading;
  curDegrees = compass.magneticHeading;

  cnv.clearRect(0,0,cnvWidth, cnvHeight);
  cnv.translate(cnvWidth/2, cnvHeight/2);
  cnv.rotate(degreeMove*Math.PI/180);
  cnv.translate(-cnvWidth/2, -cnvHeight/2);
  cnv.drawImage(img, 0, 0);
}

function fail(error)
{
```

```
        alert("Error: " + error.code);
      }
  </script>
  <style>
  #container
  {
    margin: 6px;
  }

  #compassNumerical{
    text-align: center;
    font-size: 6em;
    font-family: Arial, Verdana, sans-serif;
    font-weight: bold;
  }
  #compassRose /*img*/
  {
    /*width: 95%;*/
    width: 300px;
    height: 334px;
    margin-left: auto;
    margin-right: auto;
  }
  </style>
  <title>Scout Compass</title>
  </head>
  <body>
    <div id="container">
      <div id="compassRose">
        <canvas id="myCanvas"></canvas>
      </div>
      <div id="compassNumerical">12</div>
    </div>
  </body>
</html>
```

Example 8-11: The full code listing for the Scout Compass app.

Whack-a-Mole

Gaming and CreateJS

Ahh... carnivals. The rides, the food, the games.

We're going to create a simple iPad mini optimized game based on the carnival game Whack-a-Mole. If you're not familiar with the game, it consists of animatronic moles that pop through holes in a console. The player is charged with "whacking" them with a mallet. For the iPad mini version we're creating today, I'd recommend leaving the mallet aside and using your finger.

The game is iPad mini optimized because all of the images are sized for the iPad mini screen, which is 1024 x 768. By reoptimizing the graphics and changing the value of two variables, the game could be successfully translated to any touchscreen device.

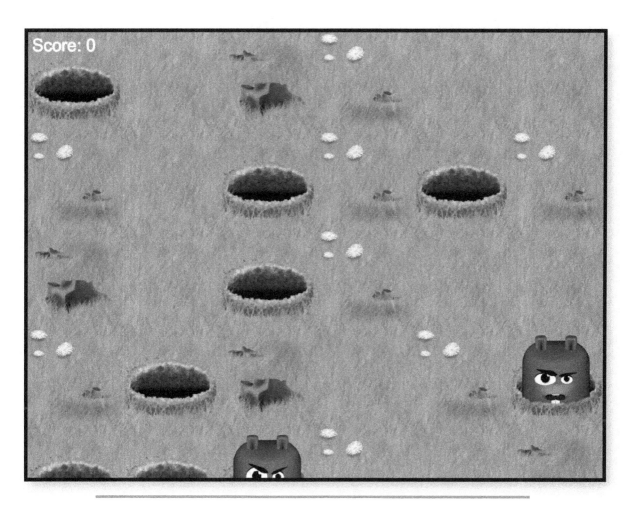

Figure 9-1: Playing Whack-a-mole with two moles waiting to be whacked. This game has three randomized levels with each becoming progressively more difficult. This game also has title screens, background music, and many of the other features you'd expect in a complete game.

Getting Ready - Creating the PhoneGap Application

In this initial section of the tutorial, we'll create a PhoneGap application and modify the template provided for our own use.

1 With PhoneGap installed, we'll now create the PhoneGap Template app. When you create a new PhoneGap application, a template app is installed by PhoneGap. This template is essentially a placeholder and most of it can be removed. To create the PhoneGap app, make sure your command line is pointed at the location where you want to save the app. I used the desktop. (You can use the **cd** command on the command line to change directories on Mac and PC.) Issue the command shown in example 9-1 to create the PhoneGap template app.

```
phonegap create whackAMole
```

Example 9-1: The command to create the "whackAMole" file.

```
<!DOCTYPE html>
<html>
  <head>
    <meta charset="utf-8" />
    <meta name="format-detection"
content="telephone=no" />
    <meta name="msapplication-tap-
highlight" content="no" />
    <!-- WARNING: for iOS 7, remove the
width=device-width and height=device-
height attributes. See https://issues.
apache.org/jira/browse/CB-4323 -->
    <meta name="viewport" content="user-
scalable=no, initial-scale=1, maximum-
scale=1, minimum-scale=1, width=device-
width, height=device-height, target-
densitydpi=device-dpi" />
    <title>Hello World</title>
    <script type="text/javascript"
src="cordova.js"></script>
  </head>
  <body>

  </body>
</html>
```

Example 9-2: The edited index.html file.

2 The command you issued created a folder called whackAMole. Open that folder and then the **www** folder inside it. Inside that folder, delete everything except config.xml and index.html. The files and folders we're deleting are for the template application that we don't need.

3 Open index.html in your text editor. There are unnecessary references to the template application in the code. Edit your code so it appears as shown in example 9-2.

Adding the Needed Libraries

We're going to be using the excellent CreateJS library to assist us with some of the heavy lifting for the game. The CreateJS library will assist with preloading game assets, animation, sound, and other aspects that would be more cumbersome to create in pure Javascript. Point your browser at https://code.createjs.com/createjs-2014.12.12.min.js. This page will provide you with a minified version of the CreateJS library. The minified version will appear almost unreadable, but is optimized for speed and efficiency.

Figure 9-2: The minified CreateJS library

```
<script type="text/javascript"
src="createjs.js"></script>
```

Example 9-3: Adding the code to include the libraries.

Copy all of the text from the minified CreateJS library and place it in a blank text document. Save that document as **createjs.js** inside the www folder created by PhoneGap. You'll need to add one line of code to the index.html file to connect the createjs library file to your code. Under the line that adds the Cordova library, add the code shown in example 9-3.

We're also going to create a number of our own additional library files. We're going to do this for two reasons:

1. We're not going to use any global variables in the code. When you're using external libraries it's a best practice to avoid global variables in order to avoid collisions with variables in the libraries themselves. Imagine what would happen if the gaming library had a variable called playerScore and you were using a variable of the same name!

2. In total, the code for this program will be over 450 lines. We're going to use the external library objects that we create to help us organize the codebase for the application.

Create blank pages with the following names and store them in the www folder:

constants.js

globals.js

game.js

display.js

We'll be using constants, globals, and display to create objects that contain properties relevant to the game. The final library file, game. js, will be the actual game logic.

To connect these libraries to our application, add the code shown in example 9-4 to the document <head> element.

```
    <script type="text/javascript"
src="constants.js"></script>
    <script type="text/javascript"
src="globals.js"></script>
    <script type="text/javascript"
src="game.js"></script>
    <script type="text/javascript"
src="display.js"></script>
```

Example 9-4: Adding the extra libraries to our code.

Adding the Assets

Assets are, of course, all of the images, files, and animations that are included in the game. We've provided the assets for you. (You may also download the assets for this game at https://s3-us-west-2.amazonaws.com/labcontent/assets.zip).

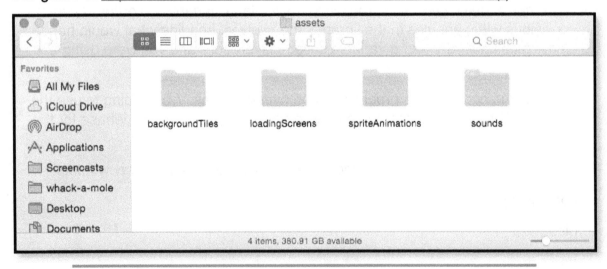

Figure 9-3: Asset folders for Whack-a-mole.

We've included four separate types of assets. Background tiles will be used to create the main playing surface. Loading Screens are 1024 x 768 screens displayed before and after the game and between each level. Sounds includes both music loops and sound effects used in the game. Sprite animations are specially prepared images that show each stage of an animation— like a mole popping up or being hit.

Figure 9-4: The sprite animation that is played when the player hits the mole. This animation lasts for approximately one second.

(A big shout out to LearnToProgram's graphic designer, Alexandria O'Brien, who created all of the graphic assets! You can give her a round of applause as you read this.)

Creating the UI

This game doesn't have a traditional PhoneGap mobile app user interface. We use the canvas element to display everything. The canvas element itself is perfect for developing games. It allows both vector-based drawing and display of bitmap graphics. CreateJS creates an abstraction of the canvas known as the stage. The concept of the stage may be familiar if you've worked with Adobe Flash or Adobe Flex in the past.

```
▸    <body>
▸        <canvas id="myCanvas"></canvas>
▸    </body>
```

Figure 9-5: Creating the canvas.

1 In our HTML we simply have to define the canvas element within the body of our document.

We've given the canvas the id "myCanvas" so it can be identified by the Javascript.

2 Since we're using the canvas for just about everything, CSS is not applied. We only have two CSS rules for our entire application (shown in example 9-5).

All this CSS does is eliminate the page margin so the canvas is right on the edge of the screen. I also turned the canvas background green in case the initial screen takes a moment to load.

You'll want to put these in a text document called mole.css and save the file in your www folder.

3 Finally, you'll want to attach the CSS your HTML with the line of code (shown in example 9-6) placed in the document <head> element.

```
body
{
    margin: 0px;
}

#myCanvas
{
    background-color: green;
}
```

Example 9-5: The two CSS rules used for this application.

```
<link href="mole.css" rel="stylesheet" />
```

Example 9-6: Attaching the CSS to the HTML file.

Creating the Game in Javascript

There is considerable code in this game. Take frequent breaks as you key it in. Some of the code is quite dense and you don't want to make mistakes that can be avoided.

1 Let's start with the constants.js file shown in example 9-7.

You can probably tell from context what these constants are used for. The reason I put values like WIDTH and HEIGHT of the gameplay area in constants is that these can be easily changed or adjusted for a bigger or smaller play surface--same with the width of the game tiles and the columns and rows of tiles on the game surface.

The last four items control the frequency that a new mole might appear (in milliseconds) and the number of seconds a level lasts. I put these here for convenience, so I could easily change them and adjust gameplay.

constants.js

```
var constant = new Object();
constant.WIDTH=1024;
constant.HEIGHT=768;
constant.TILEWIDTH= 170;
constant.TILEHEIGHT= 168;
constant.COLUMNS = 6;
constant.ROWS = 5;
constant.LEVEL1FREQUENCY = 33;
constant.LEVEL2FREQUENCY = 26;
constant.LEVEL3FREQUENCY = 19;
constant.LEVELTIME = 20
```

Example 9-7: The Javascript file that defines a number of constants in the game.

Note that all of these constants are contained in the Javascript object constant. We can access them anywhere in the code with the dot notation. For example, to access LEVELTIME, we'd write constant.LEVELTIME.

2 Next we have our global object as shown in example 9-8.

These are variables I will likely need in more than one function. As I explained a bit earlier, I wanted to completely avoid using global variables in this game, so I created a global object.

These are stored in globals.js.

3 Our final object is the display object (display.js). This is another global object, but I wanted to encapsulate it separately from the globals since all of these are objects that are displayed on the stage.

globals.js

```
var globals = new Object();
globals.level = 1;
globals.gameIntv = null;
globals.playing = false;
globals.gameTime = 0;
globals.holePositions= null;
globals.score = 0;
globals.scoreText = null;
```

Example 9-8: The code to create a global object.

display.js

```
var display = new Object();
display.stage = null;
display.queue = null;
display.hitAnimation = null;
display.idleAnimation = null;
display.laughingAnimation = null;
display.popAnimation = null;
display.teaseAnimation = null;
```

Example 9-9: The display object.

Finally, of course, we have our game logic. This is stored in a file called game.js.

game.js

```
//
//
window.onload=function()
{
  init();
  //document.addEventListener('deviceready', init, false);
}

function init()
{
  setupCanvas();
  preloadAssets();
}

function preloadAssets()
{
  display.queue = new createjs.LoadQueue();
  display.queue.installPlugin(createjs.Sound);
  display.queue.on("complete" , assetsLoaded, this);
  display.queue.loadManifest([
    {id: "ls_title", src:"assets/loadingScreens/ls_title.jpg"},
    {id: "ls_credit", src:"assets/loadingScreens/ls_credit.jpg"},
    {id: "ls_gameOver", src:"assets/loadingScreens/ls_gameOver.jpg"},
    {id: "ls_level1", src:"assets/loadingScreens/ls_level1.jpg"},
    {id: "ls_level2", src:"assets/loadingScreens/ls_level2.jpg"},
    {id: "ls_level3", src:"assets/loadingScreens/ls_level3.jpg"},
    {id: "ls_winner", src:"assets/loadingScreens/ls_winner.jpg"},
    {id: "bt_grass", src:"assets/backgroundTiles/bt_grass.png"},
    {id: "bt_hole", src:"assets/backgroundTiles/bt_hole.png"},
    {id: "bt_flowerRock", src:"assets/backgroundTiles/bt_flowerRock.png"},
    {id: "bt_rock", src:"assets/backgroundTiles/bt_rock.png"},
    {id: "bt_flowers", src:"assets/backgroundTiles/bt_flowers.png"},
    {id: "snd_welcome", src:"assets/sounds/welcome.mp3"},
    {id: "snd_punch", src:"assets/sounds/punch.mp3"},
    {id: "snd_level1Background", src:"assets/sounds/circus1.mp3"},
    {id: "snd_level2Background", src:"assets/sounds/circus2.mp3"},
```

```
      {id: "snd_level3Background", src:"assets/sounds/circus3.mp3"},
      {id: "snd_laugh", src:"assets/sounds/laugh.mp3"},
      {id: "ss_hit", src:"assets/spriteAnimations/spritesheet_hit.png"},
      {id: "ss_idle", src:"assets/spriteAnimations/spritesheet_idle.png"},
      {id: "ss_laughing", src:"assets/spriteAnimations/spritesheet_laughing.png"},
      {id: "ss_pop", src:"assets/spriteAnimations/spritesheet_pop.png"},
      {id: "ss_tease", src:"assets/spriteAnimations/spritesheet_tease.png"}

  ]);
}

function assetsLoaded()
{
  //Display the Level1 Screen
  var background = display.queue.getResult("ls_title");
  display.stage.addChild(new createjs.Bitmap(background));
  display.stage.update();

  //Register Sprite Sheets
  registerSpriteSheets();

  //click to start the game
  display.stage.addEventListener("click", function(event) { loadLevel(); })

  //Play welcome music
  createjs.Sound.play("snd_welcome");
}

function registerSpriteSheets()
{
  //Hit Spritesheet
  var data = {
    images: [display.queue.getResult("ss_hit")],
    frames: {width:170, height: 168},
    animations: { hit: [0,6] } , framerate: 10
  };

  var hitSpriteSheet = new createjs.SpriteSheet(data);
  display.hitAnimation = new createjs.Sprite(hitSpriteSheet, "hit");

  //Idle Spritesheet
```

```
    var data = {
      images: [display.queue.getResult("ss_idle")],
      frames: {width:170, height: 168},
      animations: { idle: [0,6] } , framerate: 10
    };

    var idleSpriteSheet = new createjs.SpriteSheet(data);
    display.idleAnimation = new createjs.Sprite(idleSpriteSheet, "idle");

    //Laughing Spritesheet
    var data = {
      images: [display.queue.getResult("ss_laughing")],
      frames: {width:170, height: 168},
      animations: { laugh: [0,12] } , framerate: 10
    };

    var laughingSpriteSheet = new createjs.SpriteSheet(data);
    display.laughingAnimation = new createjs.Sprite(laughingSpriteSheet, "laugh");

    //Pop Animation
    var data = {
      images: [display.queue.getResult("ss_pop")],
      frames: {width:170, height: 168},
      animations: { pop: [0,5] } , framerate: 10
    };

    var popSpriteSheet = new createjs.SpriteSheet(data);
    display.popAnimation = new createjs.Sprite(popSpriteSheet, "pop");

    //Tease Animation
    var data = {
      images: [display.queue.getResult("ss_tease")],
      frames: {width:170, height: 168},
      animations: { tease: [0,13] } , framerate: 10
    };

    var teaseSpriteSheet = new createjs.SpriteSheet(data);
    display.teaseAnimation = new createjs.Sprite(teaseSpriteSheet, "tease");

  }
```

```
function loadLevel()
{
  //Stop Sounds
  createjs.Sound.stop();

  //Remove Current Click Listener
  display.stage.removeAllEventListeners();

  //Display Level Screen
  display.stage.removeAllChildren();
  display.stage.update();
  var levelLabel = "ls_level" + globals.level;
  var level_screen = display.queue.getResult(levelLabel);
  display.stage.addChild(new createjs.Bitmap(level_screen));
  display.stage.update();

  //Play Level Music
  var music = "snd_level" + globals.level + "Background";
  createjs.Sound.play(music,{loop:8});

  //Wait for click to start play
  display.stage.addEventListener("click", function(event) { startLevel(); })

}

function startLevel()
{
  //Remove Level Screen
  display.stage.removeAllChildren();
  display.stage.removeAllEventListeners();

  //Display the Level Grid
  var levelGrid = createLevelGrid(constant.COLUMNS, constant.ROWS);
  displayLevelGrid(levelGrid, constant.COLUMNS, constant.ROWS);

  //Make a simple array of hole positions
  globals.holePositions = new Array();
  for(x=0; x < levelGrid.length; x++)
  {
    for(y=0; y < levelGrid[x].length; y++)
    {
      if(levelGrid[x][y] == "bt_hole")
```

```
          {
            globals.holePositions.push(x);
            globals.holePositions.push(y);
          }
        }
      }

    //start ticker
    createjs.Ticker.setFPS(15);
    createjs.Ticker.addEventListener('tick', display.stage);
    createjs.Ticker.addEventListener('tick', playLoop);
    globals.playing = true;
    playGame(globals.holePositions);
  }


  function playLoop()
  {

    if(globals.playing)
    {
      globals.gameTime = globals.gameTime + (1/15);

      if(globals.gameTime < constant.LEVELTIME)
      {
        //How Hard will the level be?
        if(globals.level == 1)
        {
          var frequency = constant.LEVEL1FREQUENCY;
        } else if (globals.level == 2)
        {
          var frequency = constant.LEVEL2FREQUENCY;
        } else
        {
          var frequency = constant.LEVEL3FREQUENCY;
        }
        //If the numbers match-- create a mole
        var match = Math.floor((Math.random() * frequency) + 0);
        if(match == 1)
        {
          createRandomMole();
        }
```

```
      } else

    {
      globals.playing = false;
      endLevel();
    }
  }
}

function createRandomMole()
{
  var numHoles = globals.holePositions.length/2;
  var where = Math.floor((Math.random() * globals.holePositions.length) + 0);   //
Where will the mole appear?
      if(where % 2 != 0)
      {
        where--;
      }

      var y = globals.holePositions[where];
      var x = globals.holePositions[where+1];

      //Mole pops up
      display.popAnimation.x = x * constant.TILEWIDTH;
      display.popAnimation.y = y * constant.TILEHEIGHT;
      display.popAnimation.play();
      display.stage.addChild(display.popAnimation);
      display.stage.update();

      //Should the mole laugh at the player
      var playSound = Math.floor((Math.random() * 4) + 0);
      if (playSound ==3) { createjs.Sound.play("snd_laugh"); }

      //After the mole pops up run a secondary animation
      display.popAnimation.on("animationend", function(){
        //which mole
        var which = Math.floor((Math.random() * 2) + 0);
        if(which == 0) { var mole = display.laughingAnimation }
        else if (which ==1 ) {var mole = display.idleAnimation }
        else {var mole = display.teaseAnimation };
```

```
            //display the mole in the proper location
            display.stage.removeChild(display.popAnimation);
            mole.y = y * constant.TILEWIDTH;
            mole.x = x * constant.TILEWIDTH;
            mole.play();
            display.stage.addChild(mole);
            display.stage.update();
            mole.addEventListener("click", hit, false);  //What to do if the mole is
    "hit"
        });
    }

    function hit(mole)
    {
      //Play a sound, and display the "hit" animation
      createjs.Sound.play("snd_punch");
      display.stage.removeChild(mole.target);
      globals.score = globals.score + 10;
      display.hitAnimation.x = mole.target.x;
      display.hitAnimation.y = mole.target.y;
      display.stage.addChild(display.hitAnimation);
      display.stage.update();
      displayScore();

      //When the animation is done, remove it
      display.hitAnimation.on("animationend", function(){
        display.stage.removeChild(display.hitAnimation);
      });
    }

    function playGame()
    {
      globals.playing = true;
      globals.gameTime = 0;
      displayScore();

    }

    function endLevel()
    {
      clearInterval(globals.gameIntv);
      if(globals.level < 3)
```

```
    {
      globals.level++;
      loadLevel();
    } else
    {
      gameOver();
    }
  }

  function gameOver()
  {
    //Stop Sounds
    createjs.Sound.stop();

    //Remove Current Click Listener
    display.stage.removeAllEventListeners();

    //Display Level Screen
    display.stage.removeAllChildren();
    display.stage.update();

    var background = display.queue.getResult("ls_gameOver");
    display.stage.addChild(new createjs.Bitmap(background));
    display.stage.update();

    //Play welcome music
    createjs.Sound.play("snd_welcome");

    display.stage.addEventListener("click", function() {
      globals.level = 1;
      loadLevel();
      globals.score = 0;

    } );
  }

  function displayLevelGrid(levelGrid, colsNumber, rowsNumber)
  {
    //Where will the tile be positioned?
    var xPos=0;
    var yPos=0;
```

```
    for(var x = 0; x < rowsNumber; x++)
    {
      xPos = 0;
      for(var y =0; y < colsNumber; y++)
      {
        var tile = display.queue.getResult(levelGrid[x][y]);

        //Display the tile in the correct position
        var bitmap = new createjs.Bitmap(tile);
        bitmap.x = xPos;
        bitmap.y = yPos;
        display.stage.addChild(bitmap);

        //Position for next tile on the X-axis
        xPos += constant.TILEWIDTH;
      }

      //Position for the next tile on the Y-axis
      yPos += constant.TILEHEIGHT;
    }

  }

  function displayScore()
  {
    display.stage.removeChild(globals.scoreText);
    globals.scoreText = new createjs.Text("Score: " + globals.score . "30px Arial".
  "#ffffff");
    globals.scoreText.y = 10;
    globals.scoreText.x = 10;
    display.stage.addChild(globals.scoreText);
    display.stage.update();
  }

  function createLevelGrid(colsNumber, rowsNumber)
  {
    var levelGrid= new Array();

    //Each Row
    for(var x=0; x < rowsNumber; x++)
      {
        var row = new Array();
```

```
      //Each column in that row
      for(var y = 0; y < colsNumber; y++)
      {
        var tileType = Math.floor((Math.random() * 4) + 0);

        //Associate Graphic with numerical tileType
        if(tileType ==0)
        {
          tileType = "bt_grass";
        } else if (tileType ==1)
        {
          tileType = "bt_hole";
        } else if (tileType ==2)
        {
          tileType = "bt_flowerRock";
        } else if (tileType ==3)
        {
          tileType = "bt_rock";
        } else
        {
          tileType = "bt_flowers";
        }
        row[y] = tileType;
      }
      levelGrid[x] = row;
    }
  return levelGrid;
}


function setupCanvas()
{
  display.stage = new createjs.Stage("myCanvas");
  display.stage.canvas.width = constant.WIDTH;
  display.stage.canvas.height = constant.HEIGHT;
}
```

Figure 9-6: The code to define the game logic operations.

I've tried to put a somewhat generous number of comments in the code so you can follow what's going on in each function.

Understanding the Gameplay

The initialization sequence is fairly extensive for this app:

```
window.onload=function()
{
  init();
  //document.addEventListener('deviceready', init, false);
}

function init()
{
  setupCanvas();
  preloadAssets();
}

function preloadAssets()
{
  display.queue = new createjs.LoadQueue();
  display.queue.installPlugin(createjs.Sound);
  display.queue.on("complete" , assetsLoaded, this);
  display.queue.loadManifest([
    {id: "ls_title", src:"assets/loadingScreens/ls_title.jpg"},
    {id: "ls_credit", src:"assets/loadingScreens/ls_credit.jpg"},
    {id: "ls_gameOver", src:"assets/loadingScreens/ls_gameOver.jpg"},
    {id: "ls_level1", src:"assets/loadingScreens/ls_level1.jpg"},
    {id: "ls_level2", src:"assets/loadingScreens/ls_level2.jpg"},
    {id: "ls_level3", src:"assets/loadingScreens/ls_level3.jpg"},
    {id: "ls_winner", src:"assets/loadingScreens/ls_winner.jpg"},
    {id: "bt_grass", src:"assets/backgroundTiles/bt_grass.png"},
    {id: "bt_hole", src:"assets/backgroundTiles/bt_hole.png"},
    {id: "bt_flowerRock", src:"assets/backgroundTiles/bt_flowerRock.png"},
    {id: "bt_rock", src:"assets/backgroundTiles/bt_rock.png"},
    {id: "bt_flowers", src:"assets/backgroundTiles/bt_flowers.png"},
    {id: "snd_welcome", src:"assets/sounds/welcome.mp3"},
    {id: "snd_punch", src:"assets/sounds/punch.mp3"},
    {id: "snd_level1Background", src:"assets/sounds/circus1.mp3"},
    {id: "snd_level2Background", src:"assets/sounds/circus2.mp3"},
    {id: "snd_level3Background", src:"assets/sounds/circus3.mp3"},
    {id: "snd_laugh", src:"assets/sounds/laugh.mp3"},
```

```
▸     {id: "ss_hit", src:"assets/spriteAnimations/spritesheet_hit.png"},
▸     {id: "ss_idle", src:"assets/spriteAnimations/spritesheet_idle.png"},
▸     {id: "ss_laughing", src:"assets/spriteAnimations/spritesheet_laughing.png"},
▸     {id: "ss_pop", src:"assets/spriteAnimations/spritesheet_pop.png"},
▸     {id: "ss_tease", src:"assets/spriteAnimations/spritesheet_tease.png"}
▸
▸  ]);
▸ }
```

Example 9-10: The initialization sequence for this game.

Our init() function calls a first function that sets up the Canvas for use as shown in example 9-11.

We're using the constants from the constants.js file (and object contained within) to set the width and height of the stage. Notice how the canvas now becomes a property of the stage object itself. The stage itself is part of the display object created in display.js. Once this code has run, our canvas is ready for use.

```
▸  function setupCanvas()
▸  {
▸    display.stage = new createjs.
   Stage("myCanvas");
▸    display.stage.canvas.width = constant.
   WIDTH;
▸    display.stage.canvas.height = constant.
   HEIGHT;
▸  }
```

Example 9-11: The setupCanvas() function.

The balance of the initialization code sets up a manifest of assets that need to be loaded into the game. Each is given a unique id that will be used to call the asset later on. The assetsLoaded() function is delegated to run once the assets are loaded. The line of code shown in example 9-12 facilitates that process.

```
▸  display.queue.on("complete" , assetsLoaded,
   this);
```

Example 9-12: The assetsLoaded() function runs once the assets are finished loading.

We need to use a delegate in this case because it's impossible to predict how long it will take the assets to load—and we need the assets to be fully loaded before continuing.

```
function assetsLoaded()
{
    //Display the Level1 Screen
    var background = display.queue.getResult("ls_title");
    display.stage.addChild(new createjs.Bitmap(background));
    display.stage.update();

    //Register Sprite Sheets
    registerSpriteSheets();

    //click to start the game
    display.stage.addEventListener("click", function(event) { loadLevel(); })

    //Play welcome music
    createjs.Sound.play("snd_welcome");
}

function registerSpriteSheets()
{
    //Hit Spritesheet
    var data = {
        images: [display.queue.getResult("ss_hit")],
        frames: {width:170, height: 168},
        animations: { hit: [0,6] } , framerate: 10
    };

    var hitSpriteSheet = new createjs.SpriteSheet(data);
    display.hitAnimation = new createjs.Sprite(hitSpriteSheet, "hit");

    //Idle Spritesheet
    var data = {
        images: [display.queue.getResult("ss_idle")],
        frames: {width:170, height: 168},
        animations: { idle: [0,6] } , framerate: 10
    };

    var idleSpriteSheet = new createjs.SpriteSheet(data);
    display.idleAnimation = new createjs.Sprite(idleSpriteSheet, "idle");
```

```
    //Laughing Spritesheet
    var data = {
      images: [display.queue.getResult("ss_laughing")],
      frames: {width:170, height: 168},
      animations: { laugh: [0,12] } , framerate: 10
    };

    var laughingSpriteSheet = new createjs.SpriteSheet(data);
    display.laughingAnimation = new createjs.Sprite(laughingSpriteSheet, "laugh");

    //Pop Animation
    var data = {
      images: [display.queue.getResult("ss_pop")],
      frames: {width:170, height: 168},
      animations: { pop: [0,5] } , framerate: 10
    };

    var popSpriteSheet = new createjs.SpriteSheet(data);
    display.popAnimation = new createjs.Sprite(popSpriteSheet, "pop");

    //Tease Animation
    var data = {
      images: [display.queue.getResult("ss_tease")],
      frames: {width:170, height: 168},
      animations: { tease: [0,13] } , framerate: 10
    };

    var teaseSpriteSheet = new createjs.SpriteSheet(data);
    display.teaseAnimation = new createjs.Sprite(teaseSpriteSheet, "tease");

}
```

Example 9-13: The assetsLoaded() function.

The first thing assetsLoaded() does is display the title page on the stage. Keep in mind that all interactions with the stage are queued until the update() function is run. Next the registerSpriteSheet() function is called. This function provides the necessary data about each spritesheet and then loads each spritesheet and animation into a sprite that can be displayed on the stage.

For each spritesheet we indicate the image file (which comes from the manifest), the width and height of the frames, and the animations. You can create a spritesheet with multiple animations, but for simplicity's sake, we made only one animation per spritesheet.

After registering the spritesheets, assetsLoaded() creates a click listener that continues the game by calling loadLevel() when the stage is clicked. Finally background music is played for the user using createJS.Sound().

The action continues with the loadlLevel() function:

```
function loadLevel()
{
  //Stop Sounds
  createjs.Sound.stop();

  //Remove Current Click Listener
  display.stage.removeAllEventListeners();

  //Display Level Screen
  display.stage.removeAllChildren();
  display.stage.update();
  var levelLabel = "ls_level" + globals.level;
  var level_screen = display.queue.getResult(levelLabel);
  display.stage.addChild(new createjs.Bitmap(level_screen));
  display.stage.update();

  //Play Level Music
  var music = "snd_level" + globals.level + "Background";
  createjs.Sound.play(music.{loop:8});

  //Wait for click to start play
  display.stage.addEventListener("click". function(event) { startLevel(); })

}

function startLevel()
{
  //Remove Level Screen
  display.stage.removeAllChildren();
  display.stage.removeAllEventListeners();
```

```
//Display the Level Grid
var levelGrid = createLevelGrid(constant.COLUMNS, constant.ROWS);
displayLevelGrid(levelGrid, constant.COLUMNS, constant.ROWS);

//Make a simple array of hole positions
globals.holePositions = new Array();
for(x=0; x < levelGrid.length; x++)ca
{
  for(y=0; y < levelGrid[x].length; y++)
  {
    if(levelGrid[x][y] == "bt_hole")
    {
      globals.holePositions.push(x);
      globals.holePositions.push(y);
    }
  }
}

//start ticker
createjs.Ticker.setFPS(15);
createjs.Ticker.addEventListener('tick', display.stage);
createjs.Ticker.addEventListener('tick', playLoop);
globals.playing = true;
playGame(globals.holePositions);
}
```

Example 9-14: The loadLevel() function.

loadlevel() and helper function startLevel() are primarily tasked with setting up the level and the game board by randomizing the placement of the tiles on the board. You'll remember there are five different background tiles; those tiles need to be arranged on the grid. The createLevelGrid() function randomizes the placement of tiles across the grid. The displayLevelGrid() actually displays the tiles in place. The final part of startLevel() starts the game timer at 15 frames per second and creates a callback that updates the display.stage object and runs the playLoop function (which controls the gameplay). The globals.playing flag is set to true and the game begins with the playGame() function.

```
function createLevelGrid(colsNumber,
rowsNumber)
{
  var levelGrid= new Array();

  //Each Row
  for(var x=0; x < rowsNumber; x++)
    {
      var row = new Array();
      //Each column in that row
      for(var y = 0; y < colsNumber; y++)
        {
          var tileType = Math.floor((Math.
random() * 4) + 0);

          //Associate Graphic with numerical
tileType
          if(tileType ==0)
          {
            tileType = "bt_grass";
          } else if (tileType ==1)
          {
            tileType = "bt_hole";
          } else if (tileType ==2)
          {
            tileType = "bt_flowerRock";
          } else if (tileType ==3)
          {
            tileType = "bt_rock";
          } else
          {
            tileType = "bt_flowers";
          }
          row[y] = tileType;
        }
      levelGrid[x] = row;
    }
  return levelGrid;
}
```

Example 9-15: createLevelGrid() is called at the start of the level.

createLevelGrid() and displayLevelGrid() are called as each level begins to create a randomized grid of tiles. This effectively makes each level and each game a little bit different.

1   createLevelGrid() (shown in example 9-15) takes a number of rows and columns as arguments and using randomization places a certain tileType in each quadrant of the grid. Since moles will only appear where there is a hole (type bt_hole) we need to track those areas and use them during the actual gameplay.

2 The grid we create is actually displayed by the function shown in example 9-16.

```
function displayLevelGrid(levelGrid,
colsNumber, rowsNumber)
{
  //Where will the tile be positioned?
  var xPos=0;
  var yPos=0;

  for(var x = 0; x < rowsNumber; x++)
  {
    xPos = 0;
    for(var y =0; y < colsNumber; y++)
    {
      var tile = display.queue.
getResult(levelGrid[x][y]);

      //Display the tile in the correct
position
      var bitmap = new createjs.
Bitmap(tile);
      bitmap.x = xPos;
      bitmap.y = yPos;
      display.stage.addChild(bitmap);

      //Position for next tile on the
X-axis
      xPos += constant.TILEWIDTH;
    }

    //Position for the next tile on the
Y-axis
    yPos += constant.TILEHEIGHT;
  }

}
```

Example 9-16: Once the grid is created the grid is displayed.

```
    function playGame()
    {
      globals.playing = true;
      globals.gameTime = 0;
      displayScore();

    }
```

playGame() starts our level off by resetting the gameTime to zero and displaying the current score.

Example 9-17: The playGame() function.

However the heart of the game is the game loop which is being called by the game timer we set up earlier. We selected a rate of play of 15 frames per second, so this game loop function will be called 15 times per second.

```
    function playLoop()
    {

      if(globals.playing)
      {
        globals.gameTime = globals.gameTime + (1/15);

        if(globals.gameTime < constant.LEVELTIME)
        {
          //How hard will the level be?
          if(globals.level == 1)
          {
            var frequency = constant.LEVEL1FREQUENCY;
          } else if (globals.level == 2)
          {
            var frequency = constant.LEVEL2FREQUENCY;
          } else
          {
            var frequency = constant.LEVEL3FREQUENCY;
          }
```

```
        //If the numbers match, create a mole
        var match = Math.floor((Math.random() * frequency) + 0);
        if(match == 1)
        {
          createRandomMole();
        }

    } else

    {
      globals.playing = false;
      endLevel();
    }
  }
}
```

Example 9-18: The playLoop() function.

First we determine if the globals.playing is true. If it is, we know that gameplay is occurring (as opposed to the player looking at a title screen, etc). With gameplay occurring, depending on the level, we're going to use a frequency factor to determine how often a mole appears. At higher levels the moles will appear more often. We use a random number match to determine whether to display a mole. If the random number generated is one, we'll call the createRandomMole() function.

```
function createRandomMole()
{
  var numHoles = globals.holePositions.length/2;
  var where = Math.floor((Math.random() * globals.holePositions.length) + 0);    //
  Where will the mole appear?
      if(where % 2 != 0)
      {
        where--;
      }

    var y = globals.holePositions[where];
    var x = globals.holePositions[where+1];

    //Mole pops up
```

```
        display.popAnimation.x = x * constant.TILEWIDTH;
        display.popAnimation.y = y * constant.TILEHEIGHT;
        display.popAnimation.play();
        display.stage.addChild(display.popAnimation);
        display.stage.update();

        //Should the mole laugh at the player
        var playSound = Math.floor((Math.random() * 4) + 0);
        if (playSound ==3) { createjs.Sound.play("snd_laugh"); }

        //After the mole pops up run a secondary animation
        display.popAnimation.on("animationend", function(){
          //which mole
          var which = Math.floor((Math.random() * 2) + 0);
          if(which == 0) { var mole = display.laughingAnimation }
          else if (which ==1 ) {var mole = display.idleAnimation }
          else {var mole = display.teaseAnimation };

          //display the mole in the proper location
          display.stage.removeChild(display.popAnimation);
          mole.y = y * constant.TILEWIDTH;
          mole.x = x * constant.TILEWIDTH;
          mole.play();
          display.stage.addChild(mole);
          display.stage.update();
          mole.addEventListener("click", hit, false);   //What to do if the mole is
  "hit"
        });
}
```

Example 9-19: The createRandomMole() function.

We convert the array of hole positions into a number line that provides the x and y positions of each hole where a mole may appear. Then at that position, we display the pop animation which shows the mole appearing out of the hole. One time in five, we'll play a sound of the mole mocking the player with a laugh. After the mole pops up, using the animationend event, we'll run one of three animations: the laughing animation, the idle animation, or the tease animation. This is simply to provide some variety in the visuals for the player. We'll update the stage and add a click listener to the mole. If the user clicks—or, more accurately, taps—the mole, the hit() function will run.

The hit function receives an object representing the mole that has been hit. We play a punching sound, increase the score, and remove the mole animation, replacing it with the "hit" animation which shows the mole descending back into the hole. We again use the "animationend" event to remove the animation once it has completed.

A couple additional functions clean up when levels or the game itself has ended.

```
function hit(mole)
{
  //Play a sound, and display the "hit"
animation
  createjs.Sound.play("snd_punch");
  display.stage.removeChild(mole.target);
  globals.score = globals.score + 10;
  display.hitAnimation.x = mole.target.x;
  display.hitAnimation.y = mole.target.y;
  display.stage.addChild(display.
hitAnimation);
  display.stage.update();
  displayScore();

  //When the animation is done, remove it
  display.hitAnimation.on("animationend",
function(){
    display.stage.removeChild(display.
hitAnimation);
  });
}
```

Example 9-20: The hit() function runs when the user taps the mole.

```
function playGame()
{
  globals.playing = true;
  globals.gameTime = 0;
  displayScore();

}

function endLevel()
{
  clearInterval(globals.gameIntv);
  if(globals.level < 3)
  {
    globals.level++;
    loadLevel();
  } else
  {
    gameOver();
  }
}

function gameOver()
{
  //Stop Sounds
  createjs.Sound.stop();

  //Remove Current Click Listener
  display.stage.removeAllEventListeners();

  //Display Level Screen
  display.stage.removeAllChildren();
  display.stage.update();

  var background = display.queue.getResult("ls_gameOver");
  display.stage.addChild(new createjs.Bitmap(background));
  display.stage.update();

  //Play welcome music
  createjs.Sound.play("snd_welcome");

  display.stage.addEventListener("click", function() {
    globals.level = 1;
    loadLevel();
    globals.score = 0;

  } );
}
```

Example 9-21: A few additional functions to end the levels or the game.

Testing on a Device

Assuming your device is connected to your computer via USB cable and correctly provisioned (iOS only), you should be able to actually test on your device itself.

If you were testing on an Android device, you should be able to navigate to your project folder using the command line. Once pointed at the project folder, issue the following command:

```
► phonegap build android
```

Or, to build on iOS:

```
► phonegap build ios
```

If you have the Android SDK installed, you can also test on screen using an on-screen emulator. This can be very slow because the emulator is building a fully featured virtual Android device on top of your current operating system.

Congratulations on building this fairly complex game! We've found it to be just a bit addictive! Have fun with it.

The Full Code Listing

For your reference, here's the full code for the "Whack-a-Mole" app:

index.html

```
<!DOCTYPE html>
<!--
    Copyright (c) 2012-2014 Adobe Systems Incorporated. All rights reserved.

    Licensed to the Apache Software Foundation (ASF) under one
    or more contributor license agreements. See the NOTICE file
    distributed with this work for additional information
    regarding copyright ownership. The ASF licenses this file
    to you under the Apache License, Version 2.0 (the
    "License"); you may not use this file except in compliance
    with the License. You may obtain a copy of the License at

    http://www.apache.org/licenses/LICENSE-2.0

    Unless required by applicable law or agreed to in writing,
    software distributed under the License is distributed on an
    "AS IS" BASIS, WITHOUT WARRANTIES OR CONDITIONS OF ANY
     KIND, either express or implied. See the License for the
    specific language governing permissions and limitations
    under the License.
-->
<html>
  <head>
    <meta charset="utf-8" />
    <meta name="format-detection" content="telephone=no" />
    <meta name="msapplication-tap-highlight" content="no" />
    <!-- WARNING: for iOS 7, remove the width=device-width and height=device-height
attributes. See https://issues.apache.org/jira/browse/CB-4323 -->
    <meta name="viewport" content="user-scalable=no, initial-scale=1, maximum-
scale=1, minimum-scale=1, width=device-width, height=device-height, target-
densitydpi=device-dpi" />
    <script type="text/javascript" src="cordova.js"></script>
    <script type="text/javascript" src="createjs.js"></script>
    <script type="text/javascript" src="constants.js"></script>
```

```
<script type="text/javascript" src="globals.js"></script>
<script type="text/javascript" src="game.js"></script>
<script type="text/javascript" src="display.js"></script>
<link href="mole.css" rel="stylesheet" />
<title>Whack-a-Mole</title>
</head>
<body>
<canvas id="myCanvas"></canvas>
</body>
</html>
```

Example 9-22: The complete code listing for the index.html file.

constants.js

```
var constant = new Object();
constant.WIDTH=1024;
constant.HEIGHT=768;
constant.TILEWIDTH= 170;
constant.TILEHEIGHT= 168;
constant.COLUMNS = 6;
constant.ROWS = 5;
constant.LEVEL1FREQUENCY = 33;
constant.LEVEL2FREQUENCY = 26;
constant.LEVEL3FREQUENCY = 19;
constant.LEVELTIME = 20
```

Example 9-23: The complete code listing for the constants.js file.

globals.js

```
var globals = new Object();
globals.level = 1;
globals.gameIntv = null;
globals.playing = false;
globals.gameTime = 0;
globals.holePositions= null;
globals.score = 0;
globals.scoreText = null;
```

Example 9-24: The complete code listing for the globals.js file.

display.js

```
var display = new Object();
display.stage = null;
display.queue = null;
display.hitAnimation = null;
display.idleAnimation = null;
display.laughingAnimation = null;
display.popAnimation = null;
display.teaseAnimation = null;
```

Example 9-25: The complete code listing for the display.js file.

game.js

```
//Loads when screen is drawn
//
//
window.onload=function()
{
  init();
  //document.addEventListener('deviceready', init, false);
}

function init()
{
  setupCanvas();
  preloadAssets();
}

function preloadAssets()
{
  display.queue = new createjs.LoadQueue();
  display.queue.installPlugin(createjs.Sound);
  display.queue.on("complete" , assetsLoaded, this);
  display.queue.loadManifest([
    {id: "ls_title", src:"assets/loadingScreens/ls_title.jpg"},
    {id: "ls_credit", src:"assets/loadingScreens/ls_credit.jpg"},
    {id: "ls_gameOver", src:"assets/loadingScreens/ls_gameOver.jpg"},
    {id: "ls_level1", src:"assets/loadingScreens/ls_level1.jpg"},
    {id: "ls_level2", src:"assets/loadingScreens/ls_level2.jpg"},
    {id: "ls_level3", src:"assets/loadingScreens/ls_level3.jpg"},
    {id: "ls_winner", src:"assets/loadingScreens/ls_winner.jpg"},
    {id: "bt_grass", src:"assets/backgroundTiles/bt_grass.png"},
    {id: "bt_hole", src:"assets/backgroundTiles/bt_hole.png"},
    {id: "bt_flowerRock", src:"assets/backgroundTiles/bt_flowerRock.png"},
    {id: "bt_rock", src:"assets/backgroundTiles/bt_rock.png"},
    {id: "bt_flowers", src:"assets/backgroundTiles/bt_flowers.png"},
    {id: "snd_welcome", src:"assets/sounds/welcome.mp3"},
    {id: "snd_punch", src:"assets/sounds/punch.mp3"},
    {id: "snd_level1Background", src:"assets/sounds/circus1.mp3"},
    {id: "snd_level2Background", src:"assets/sounds/circus2.mp3"},
    {id: "snd_level3Background", src:"assets/sounds/circus3.mp3"},
    {id: "snd_laugh", src:"assets/sounds/laugh.mp3"},
```

```
        {id: "ss_hit", src:"assets/spriteAnimations/spritesheet_hit.png"},
        {id: "ss_idle", src:"assets/spriteAnimations/spritesheet_idle.png"},
        {id: "ss_laughing", src:"assets/spriteAnimations/spritesheet_laughing.png"},
        {id: "ss_pop", src:"assets/spriteAnimations/spritesheet_pop.png"},
        {id: "ss_tease", src:"assets/spriteAnimations/spritesheet_tease.png"}

    ]);
}

function assetsLoaded()
{
    //Display the Level1 Screen
    var background = display.queue.getResult("ls_title");
    display.stage.addChild(new createjs.Bitmap(background));
    display.stage.update();

    //Reister Sprite Sheets
    registerSpriteSheets();

    //click to start the game
    display.stage.addEventListener("click", function(event) { loadLevel(); })

    //Play welcome music
    createjs.Sound.play("snd_welcome");
}

function registerSpriteSheets()
{
    //Hit Spritesheet
    var data = {
      images: [display.queue.getResult("ss_hit")],
      frames: {width:170, height: 168},
      animations: { hit: [0,6] } , framerate: 10
    };

    var hitSpriteSheet = new createjs.SpriteSheet(data);
    display.hitAnimation = new createjs.Sprite(hitSpriteSheet, "hit");

    //Idle Spritesheet
    var data = {
      images: [display.queue.getResult("ss_idle")],
```

```
      frames: {width:170, height: 168},
      animations: { idle: [0,6] } , framerate: 10
    };

  var idleSpriteSheet = new createjs.SpriteSheet(data);
  display.idleAnimation = new createjs.Sprite(idleSpriteSheet, "idle");

  //Laughing Spritesheet
  var data = {
    images: [display.queue.getResult("ss_laughing")],
    frames: {width:170, height: 168},
    animations: { laugh: [0,12] } , framerate: 10
  };

  var laughingSpriteSheet = new createjs.SpriteSheet(data);
  display.laughingAnimation = new createjs.Sprite(laughingSpriteSheet, "laugh");

  //Pop Animation
  var data = {
    images: [display.queue.getResult("ss_pop")],
    frames: {width:170, height: 168},
    animations: { pop: [0,5] } , framerate: 10
  };

  var popSpriteSheet = new createjs.SpriteSheet(data);
  display.popAnimation = new createjs.Sprite(popSpriteSheet, "pop");

  //Tease Animation
  var data = {
    images: [display.queue.getResult("ss_tease")],
    frames: {width:170, height: 168},
    animations: { tease: [0,13] } , framerate: 10
  };

  var teaseSpriteSheet = new createjs.SpriteSheet(data);
  display.teaseAnimation = new createjs.Sprite(teaseSpriteSheet, "tease");

}

function loadLevel()
{
  //Stop Sounds
```

```
    createjs.Sound.stop();

    //Remove Current Click Listener
    display.stage.removeAllEventListeners();

    //Display Level Screen
    display.stage.removeAllChildren();
    display.stage.update();
    var levelLabel = "ls_level" + globals.level;
    var level_screen = display.queue.getResult(levelLabel);
    display.stage.addChild(new createjs.Bitmap(level_screen));
    display.stage.update();

    //Play Level Music
    var music = "snd_level" + globals.level + "Background";
    createjs.Sound.play(music,{loop:8});

    //Wait for click to start play
    display.stage.addEventListener("click", function(event) { startLevel(); })

}

function startLevel()
{
    //Remove Level Screen
    display.stage.removeAllChildren();
    display.stage.removeAllEventListeners();

    //Display the Level Grid
    var levelGrid = createLevelGrid(constant.COLUMNS, constant.ROWS);
    displayLevelGrid(levelGrid, constant.COLUMNS, constant.ROWS);

    //Make a simple array of hole positions
    globals.holePositions = new Array();
    for(x=0; x < levelGrid.length; x++)
    {
      for(y=0; y < levelGrid[x].length; y++)
      {
        if(levelGrid[x][y] == "bt_hole")
        {
          globals.holePositions.push(x);
```

```
        globals.holePositions.push(y);
      }
    }
  }

  //start ticker
  createjs.Ticker.setFPS(15);
  createjs.Ticker.addEventListener('tick', display.stage);
  createjs.Ticker.addEventListener('tick', playLoop);
  globals.playing = true;
  playGame(globals.holePositions);
}


function playLoop()
{

  if(globals.playing)
  {
    globals.gameTime = globals.gameTime + (1/15);

    if(globals.gameTime < constant.LEVELTIME)
    {
      //How Hard will the level be?
      if(globals.level == 1)
      {
        var frequency = constant.LEVEL1FREQUENCY;
      } else if (globals.level == 2)
      {
        var frequency = constant.LEVEL2FREQUENCY;
      } else
      {
        var frequency = constant.LEVEL3FREQUENCY;
      }
      //If the numbers match-- create a mole
      var match = Math.floor((Math.random() * frequency) + 0);
      if(match == 1)
      {
        createRandomMole();
      }
    } else
```

```
          {
            globals.playing = false;
            endLevel();
          }
        }
      }

    function createRandomMole()
    {
      var numHoles = globals.holePositions.length/2;
      var where = Math.floor((Math.random() * globals.holePositions.length) + 0);    //
    Where will the mole appear?
          if(where % 2 != 0)
          {
            where--;
          }

          var y = globals.holePositions[where];
          var x = globals.holePositions[where+1];

          //Mole pops up
          display.popAnimation.x = x * constant.TILEWIDTH;
          display.popAnimation.y = y * constant.TILEHEIGHT;
          display.popAnimation.play();
          display.stage.addChild(display.popAnimation);
          display.stage.update();

          //Should the mole laugh at the player
          var playSound = Math.floor((Math.random() * 4) + 0);
          if (playSound ==3) { createjs.Sound.play("snd_laugh"); }

          //After the mole pops up run a secondary animation
          display.popAnimation.on("animationend", function(){
            //which mole
            var which = Math.floor((Math.random() * 2) + 0);
            if(which == 0) { var mole = display.laughingAnimation }
            else if (which ==1 ) {var mole = display.idleAnimation }
            else {var mole = display.teaseAnimation };

            //display the mole in the proper location
            display.stage.removeChild(display.popAnimation);
```

```
          mole.y = y * constant.TILEWIDTH;
          mole.x = x * constant.TILEWIDTH;
          mole.play();
          display.stage.addChild(mole);
          display.stage.update();
          mole.addEventListener("click", hit, false);    //What to do if the mole is
    "hit"
        });
    }

    function hit(mole)
    {
      //Play a sound, and display the "hit" animation
      createjs.Sound.play("snd_punch");
      display.stage.removeChild(mole.target);
      globals.score = globals.score + 10;
      display.hitAnimation.x = mole.target.x;
      display.hitAnimation.y = mole.target.y;
      display.stage.addChild(display.hitAnimation);
      display.stage.update();
      displayScore();

      //When the animation is done, remove it
      display.hitAnimation.on("animationend", function(){
        display.stage.removeChild(display.hitAnimation);
      });
    }

    function playGame()
    {
      globals.playing = true;
      globals.gameTime = 0;
      displayScore();

    }

    function endLevel()
    {
      clearInterval(globals.gameIntv);
      if(globals.level < 3)
      {
        globals.level++;
```

```
    loadLevel();
  } else
  {
    gameOver();
  }
}

function gameOver()
{
  //Stop Sounds
  createjs.Sound.stop();

  //Remove Current Click Listener
  display.stage.removeAllEventListeners();

  //Display Level Screen
  display.stage.removeAllChildren();
  display.stage.update();

  var background = display.queue.getResult("ls_gameOver");
  display.stage.addChild(new createjs.Bitmap(background));
  display.stage.update();

  //Play welcome music
  createjs.Sound.play("snd_welcome");

  display.stage.addEventListener("click", function() {
    globals.level = 1;
    loadLevel();
    globals.score = 0;

  } );
}

function displayLevelGrid(levelGrid, colsNumber, rowsNumber)
{
  //Where will the tile be positioned?
  var xPos=0;
  var yPos=0;

  for(var x = 0; x < rowsNumber; x++)
```

```
      {
        xPos = 0;
        for(var y =0; y < colsNumber; y++)
        {
          var tile = display.queue.getResult(levelGrid[x][y]);

          //Display the tile in the correct position
          var bitmap = new createjs.Bitmap(tile);
          bitmap.x = xPos;
          bitmap.y = yPos;
          display.stage.addChild(bitmap);

          //Position for next tile on the X-axis
          xPos += constant.TILEWIDTH;
        }

        //Position for the next tile on the Y-axis
        yPos += constant.TILEHEIGHT;
      }

    }

    function displayScore()
    {
      display.stage.removeChild(globals.scoreText);
      globals.scoreText = new createjs.Text("Score: " + globals.score , "30px Arial",
    "#ffffff");
      globals.scoreText.y = 10;
      globals.scoreText.x = 10;
      display.stage.addChild(globals.scoreText);
      display.stage.update();
    }

    function createLevelGrid(colsNumber, rowsNumber)
    {
      var levelGrid= new Array();

      //Each Row
      for(var x=0; x < rowsNumber; x++)
        {
          var row = new Array();
          //Each column in that row
```

```
        for(var y = 0; y < colsNumber; y++)
        {
          var tileType = Math.floor((Math.random() * 4) + 0);

          //Associate Graphic with numerical tileType
          if(tileType ==0)
          {
            tileType = "bt_grass";
          } else if (tileType ==1)
          {
            tileType = "bt_hole";
          } else if (tileType ==2)
          {
            tileType = "bt_flowerRock";
          } else if (tileType ==3)
          {
            tileType = "bt_rock";
          } else
          {
            tileType = "bt_flowers";
          }
          row[y] = tileType;
        }
        levelGrid[x] = row;
      }
   return levelGrid;
 }


function setupCanvas()
 {
   display.stage = new createjs.Stage("myCanvas");
   display.stage.canvas.width = constant.WIDTH;
   display.stage.canvas.height = constant.HEIGHT;
 }
```

Example 9-26: The complete code listing for the game.js file.

Bat Hunt

Gaming and CreatJS

Who doesn't enjoy a good bat hunt?

We're going to create a simple iPad mini optimized game based on the Nintendo classic DuckHunt™. In the game itself, the player will try to shoot the bat using the simple touch interface. If successful, the player's score increases and a new bat is generated. If the player misses, they lose points.

The game is iPad mini optimized because all of the images are sized for the iPad mini screen, which is 1024 x 768. By reoptimizing the graphics and changing the value of two variables, the game could be successfully translated to any touchscreen device.

Figure 10-1: Playing bat hunt. The cross hair is only visible for a second after the player "shoots."

Getting Ready - Creating the PhoneGap Application

In this initial section of the tutorial we'll create a PhoneGap application and modify the template provided for our own use.

1 With PhoneGap installed, we'll now create the PhoneGap Template app. When you create a new PhoneGap application, a template app is installed by PhoneGap. This template is essentially a placeholder and most of it can be removed. To create the PhoneGap app, make sure your command line is pointed at the location where you want to save the app. I used the desktop. (You can use the **cd** command on the command line to change directories on Mac and PC.) Issue the command shown in example 10-1 to create the PhoneGap template app.

```
phonegap create batHunt
```

Example 10-1: The command to create the "batHunt" template app.

```
<!DOCTYPE html>
<html>
  <head>
    <meta charset="utf-8" />
    <meta name="format-detection"
content="telephone=no" />
    <meta name="msapplication-tap-
highlight" content="no" />
    <!-- WARNING: for iOS 7, remove the
width=device-width and height=device-
height attributes. See https://issues.
apache.org/jira/browse/CB-4323 -->
    <meta name="viewport" content="user-
scalable=no, initial-scale=1, maximum-
scale=1, minimum-scale=1, width=device-
width, height=device-height, target-
densitydpi=device-dpi" />
    <title>Hello World</title>
    <script type="text/javascript"
src="cordova.js"></script>
  </head>
  <body>
```

Example 10-2: The edited index.html file.

2 The command you issued created a folder called batHunt. Open that folder and then the **www** folder inside it. Inside that folder, delete everything except config.xml and index.html. The files and folders we're deleting are for the template application that we don't need.

3 Open index.html in your text editor. There are unnecessary references to the template application in the code. Edit your code so it appears as shown in example 10-2.

Adding Needed Libraries

We're going to be using a few free external libraries to create our game. We've supplied these for you, and they are free to download. Example 10-3 shows the includes.

```
<script language="javascript" type="text/
javascript" src="http://code.createjs.com/
createjs-2013.12.12.min.js" ></script>
<script language="javascript" type="text/
javascript" src="fastclick.js"></script>
<script language="javascript" type="text/
javascript" src="init.js" ></script>
```

Example 10-3: Linking the code to a few free external libraries for our game.

Note that the final include for init.js is going to be the file where we write our own code. You may want to create a blank file and save it in your www folder as init.js. Of the other libraries, the first is CreateJS. This library has a number of optimizations that are useful for gaming, including an asset preloader and animation system. The CreateJS library will do some of the "heavy lifting" for us. We've linked to the hosted CDN (Content Delivery Network) version of CreateJS. You may want to download the library and store it locally on the device.

We won't interact with the FastClick.js library directly, but it will be of great benefit to the user. The FastClick library defeats the normal 500 millisecond delay between the time when the user taps the screen and the program reacts. While unnoticeable in many other types of applications, in this type of game where the accuracy of a tap is critical, the delay would prove frustrating.

Figure 10-2: The game makes extensive use of the CreateJS library which makes working with elements such as spritesheets, sprites, and sounds easier.

Creating the UI

There is no UI created through HTML for this app.

The purpose of the HTML file is to provide a load page for PhoneGap. The HTML has a single display element: the canvas on which the game is played. The HTML code is shown in example 10-4.

```
<!DOCTYPE html>
<html>
  <head>
    <title>30 Minute Game</title>
    <link href="normalize.css" type="text/
css" rel="stylesheet" />
    <script language="javascript"
type="text/javascript" src="http://code.
createjs.com/createjs-2013.12.12.min.js"
></script>
    <script language="javascript"
type="text/javascript" src="init.js" ></
script>
  </head>
  <body>
    <canvas id="myCanvas"></canvas>
  </body>
</html>
```

Example 10-4: The simple HTML file.

As you can see, the HTML does little but provide scaffolding for the project. We link to several code sources within the HTML document. First, we link to normalize.css, which is a reset stylesheet. A reset stylesheet is designed to ameliorate minor differences between the browsers' rendering styles by setting the baseline for most style rules to zero.

Next, you'll see the includes that we discussed previously.

The body of the document contains the lone <canvas> element where all of the action will take place in the game.

Creating the Game in Javascript

Because of its length and complexity, we've separated out the Javascript into its own file called init.js. There is a lot of Javascript here, so be careful! Perhaps take a short break after you type each function so you can avoid making mistakes!

```javascript
var context;
var queue;
var WIDTH = 1024;
var HEIGHT = 768;
var batImage;
var stage;
var animation;
var deathAnimation;
var spriteSheet;
var enemyXPos=100;
var enemyYPos=100;
var enemyXSpeed = 1.5;
var enemyYSpeed = 1.75;
var score = 0;
var scoreText;
var gameTimer;
var gameTime = 0;
var timerText;

window.onload = function()
{
  /*
   *    Set up the Canvas with Size and height
   *
   */
  var canvas = document.getElementById('myCanvas');
  context = canvas.getContext('2d');
  context.canvas.width = WIDTH;
  context.canvas.height = HEIGHT;
  stage = new createjs.Stage("myCanvas");

  /*
   *    Set up the Asset Queue and load sounds
   *
   */
```

```
    queue = new createjs.LoadQueue(false);
    queue.installPlugin(createjs.Sound);
    queue.on("complete", queueLoaded, this);
    createjs.Sound.alternateExtensions = ["ogg"];

    /*
     *    Create a load manifest for all assets
     *
     */
    queue.loadManifest([
      {id: 'backgroundImage', src: 'assets/background.png'},
      {id: 'crossHair', src: 'assets/crosshair.png'},
      {id: 'shot', src: 'assets/shot.mp3'},
      {id: 'background', src: 'assets/countryside.mp3'},
      {id: 'gameOverSound', src: 'assets/gameOver.mp3'},
      {id: 'tick', src: 'assets/tick.mp3'},
      {id: 'deathSound', src: 'assets/die.mp3'},
      {id: 'batSpritesheet', src: 'assets/batSpritesheet.png'},
      {id: 'batDeath', src: 'assets/batDeath.png'},
    ]);
    queue.load();

    /*
     *    Create a timer that updates once per second
     *
     */
    gameTimer = setInterval(updateTime, 1000);

  }

  function queueLoaded(event)
  {
    // Add background image
    var backgroundImage = new createjs.Bitmap(queue.getResult("backgroundImage"))
    stage.addChild(backgroundImage);

    //Add Score
    scoreText = new createjs.Text("1UP: " + score.toString(), "36px Arial", "#FFF");
    scoreText.x = 10;
    scoreText.y = 10;
    stage.addChild(scoreText);
```

```
    //Ad Timer
    timerText = new createjs.Text("Time: " + gameTime.toString(), "36px Arial",
  "#FFF");
    timerText.x = 800;
    timerText.y = 10;
    stage.addChild(timerText);

    // Play background sound
    createjs.Sound.play("background", {loop: -1});

    // Create bat spritesheet
    spriteSheet = new createjs.SpriteSheet({
      "images": [queue.getResult('batSpritesheet')],
      "frames": {"width": 198, "height": 117},
      "animations": { "flap": [0,4] }
    });

    // Create bat death spritesheet
    batDeathSpriteSheet = new createjs.SpriteSheet({
      "images": [queue.getResult('batDeath')],
      "frames": {"width": 198, "height" : 148},
      "animations": {"die": [0,7, false,1 ] }
    });

    // Create bat sprite
    createEnemy();


    // Add ticker
    createjs.Ticker.setFPS(15);
    createjs.Ticker.addEventListener('tick', stage);
    createjs.Ticker.addEventListener('tick', tickEvent);

    // Set up events AFTER the game is loaded
    window.onmousedown = handleMouseDown;
  }

  function createEnemy()
  {
      animation = new createjs.Sprite(spriteSheet, "flap");
    animation.regX = 99;
```

```
    animation.regY = 58;
    animation.x = enemyXPos;
    animation.y = enemyYPos;
    animation.gotoAndPlay("flap");
    stage.addChildAt(animation,1);
}

function batDeath()
{
  deathAnimation = new createjs.Sprite(batDeathSpriteSheet, "die");
  deathAnimation.regX = 99;
  deathAnimation.regY = 58;
  deathAnimation.x = enemyXPos;
  deathAnimation.y = enemyYPos;
  deathAnimation.gotoAndPlay("die");
  stage.addChild(deathAnimation);
}

function tickEvent()
{
    //Make sure enemy bat is within game boundaries and move enemy Bat
    if(enemyXPos < WIDTH && enemyXPos > 0)
    {
            enemyXPos += enemyXSpeed;
    } else
    {
            enemyXSpeed = enemyXSpeed * (-1);
            enemyXPos += enemyXSpeed;
    }
    if(enemyYPos < HEIGHT && enemyYPos > 0)
    {
            enemyYPos += enemyYSpeed;
    } else
    {
            enemyYSpeed = enemyYSpeed * (-1);
            enemyYPos += enemyYSpeed;
    }

    animation.x = enemyXPos;
    animation.y = enemyYPos;
```

```
    }


function handleMouseDown(event)
{

    //Display CrossHair
    crossHair = new createjs.Bitmap(queue.getResult("crossHair"));
    crossHair.x = event.clientX-45;
    crossHair.y = event.clientY-45;
    stage.addChild(crossHair);
    createjs.Tween.get(crossHair).to({alpha: 0},1000);

    //Play Gunshot sound
    createjs.Sound.play("shot");

    //Increase speed of enemy slightly
    enemyXSpeed *= 1.05;
    enemyYSpeed *= 1.06;

    //Obtain Shot position
    var shotX = Math.round(event.clientX);
    var shotY = Math.round(event.clientY);
    var spriteX = Math.round(animation.x);
    var spriteY = Math.round(animation.y);

    // Compute the X and Y distance using absolte value
    var distX = Math.abs(shotX - spriteX);
    var distY = Math.abs(shotY - spriteY);

    // Anywhere in the body or head is a hit - but not the wings
    if(distX < 30 && distY < 59 )
    {
      //Hit
      stage.removeChild(animation);
      batDeath();
      score += 100;
      scoreText.text = "1UP: " + score.toString();
      createjs.Sound.play("deathSound");

      //Make it harder next time
```

```
      enemyYSpeed *= 1.25;
      enemyXSpeed *= 1.3;

      //Create new enemy
      var timeToCreate = Math.floor((Math.random()*3500)+1);
        setTimeout(createEnemy.timeToCreate);

   } else
   {
    //Miss
    score -= 10;
    scoreText.text = "1UP: " + score.toString();

   }
 }

 function updateTime()
 {
    gameTime += 1;
    if(gameTime > 60)
    {
          //End Game and Clean up
          timerText.text = "GAME OVER";
          stage.removeChild(animation);
          stage.removeChild(crossHair);
    createjs.Sound.removeSound("background");
    var si =createjs.Sound.play("gameOverSound");
          clearInterval(gameTimer);
    }
    else
    {
          timerText.text = "Time: " + gameTime
    createjs.Sound.play("tick");
    }
```

Example 10-5: The Javascript code for this game.

Understanding the Code

The initial part of the init.js code file has a number of global variable declarations. For the sake of completeness I'll include them here, but I won't discuss them at length until we encounter them in the code listing.

1 A few of the global variables are initialized here in example 10-6 as well. For the width and height of this particular game, I set constants. Remember that we're optimizing this game for the iPad mini, however, if you wanted to optimize for a different mobile system you'd have to change the value of these constants.

2 The anonymous window. onload function has a number of important component parts. First we set up the canvas, as shown in example 10-7.

```
var context;
var queue;
var WIDTH = 1024;
var HEIGHT = 768;
var batImage;
var stage;
var animation;
var deathAnimation;
var spriteSheet;
var enemyXPos=100;
var enemyYPos=100;
var enemyXSpeed = 1.5;
var enemyYSpeed = 1.75;
var score = 0;
var scoreText;
var gameTimer;
var gameTime = 0;
var timerText;
```

Example 10-6: A few global variables defined in the code.

The CreateJS library has an object known as a stage. This may sound familiar to Actionscript programmers, as the concept is borrowed directly from the Flash world. Once we get the canvas context and width and height set to the constants expressed earlier, we instantiate the stage object. The stage object will manage the hierarchy of assets that appear on stage, as well as provide a consistent timer for our animations.

```
    var canvas = document.
  getElementById('myCanvas');
    context = canvas.getContext('2d');
    context.canvas.width = WIDTH;
    context.canvas.height = HEIGHT;
    stage = new createjs.Stage("myCanvas");
```

Example 10-7: Code that sets the canvas.

3 Next within the function triggered by the window.onload event, we'll set up our asset queue and our sound component (shown in example 10-8).

```
    queue = new createjs.LoadQueue(false);
    queue.installPlugin(createjs.Sound);
    queue.on("complete", queueLoaded, this);
    createjs.Sound.alternateExtensions =
  ["ogg"];
```

Example 10-8: The asset queue and sound component.

The asset queue allows us to preload objects all at once, which makes life easier with unpredictable server speeds. Using the queue's on() method, we've delegated the queueLoaded() function to run once the entire queue is loaded. We've also told the sound object that we have .ogg sound assets as an alternative to .mp3 files.

4 Now we'll set up the manifest, which is the list of assets we're loading into the queue itself.

You'll note that the manifest is used to load several types of different assets. Here we have .mp3 files, and .png graphics which act as both spritesheets and individual graphics that will be used in the program. The queue.load() method loads the manifest into the browser DOM.

5 The final part of the window.onload delegate function starts a timer that will be used to run the timer for the game itself.

```
queue.loadManifest([
    {id: 'backgroundImage', src: 'assets/
background.png'},
    {id: 'crossHair', src: 'assets/
crosshair.png'},
    {id: 'shot', src: 'assets/shot.mp3'},
    {id: 'background', src: 'assets/
countryside.mp3'},
    {id: 'gameOverSound', src: 'assets/
gameOver.mp3'},
    {id: 'tick', src: 'assets/tick.mp3'},
    {id: 'deathSound', src: 'assets/die.
mp3'},
    {id: 'batSpritesheet', src: 'assets/
batSpritesheet.png'},
    {id: 'batDeath', src: 'assets/
batDeath.png'},
    ]);
  queue.load();
```

Example 10-9: The list of assets to load into the queue itself.

```
gameTimer = setInterval(updateTime, 1000);
```

Example 10-10: The code that starts the game's timer function.

```
    // Add background image
    var backgroundImage = new createjs.
Bitmap(queue.getResult("backgroundImage"))
    stage.addChild(backgroundImage);

    //Add Score
    scoreText = new createjs.Text("1UP: " +
score.toString(), "36px Arial", "#FFF");
    scoreText.x = 10;
    scoreText.y = 10;
    stage.addChild(scoreText);

    //Ad Timer
    timerText = new createjs.Text("Time:
" + gameTime.toString(), "36px Arial",
"#FFF");
    timerText.x = 800;
    timerText.y = 10;
    stage.addChild(timerText);

    // Play background sound
    createjs.Sound.play("background", {loop:
-1});
```

Example 10-11: The queueLoaded() function.

6 Next we'll look at the queueLoaded() function, which runs when all the items in the manifest are loaded into the DOM. The first part of this function configures some important components for the game.

The first lines of code load the backgroundImage graphic to the stage. Note that the image first must be retrieved from the queue via queue.getResult(), and instantiated as a createjs. Bitmap object. That object can be displayed on the stage via the addChild() method.

Since the stage is designed for images and animation, the next sections of code create bitmap text objects that display the timer and the score at specified locations. Finally, a background sound--earlier loaded with the manifest--is played and looped indefinitely.

7 The next step is key. We're going to set up the spritesheet for the two animations that are used in the game. The spritesheets are designed to place all of the images that make up an animation in one place.

Figure 10-3: The bat spritesheet

Figure 10-4: The bat death spritesheet

The code to configure the spritesheets is shown in example 10-12.

Each spritesheet instance is created with information about the image from the queue, the size of the individual frames on the spritesheet, and then the animation itself. As you can see, the first animation has five frames that are 198px x 117px.

```
// Create bat spritesheet
spriteSheet = new createjs.SpriteSheet({
  "images": [queue.
getResult('batSpritesheet')],
  "frames": {"width": 198, "height":
117},
  "animations": { "flap": [0,4] }
});

// Create bat death spritesheet
batDeathSpriteSheet = new createjs.
SpriteSheet({
  "images": [queue.
getResult('batDeath')],
  "frames": {"width": 198, "height" :
148},
  "animations": {"die": [0,7, false,1 ] }
});
```

Example 10-12: The code to configure the spritesheets.

```
▸   function createEnemy()
▸   {
▸     animation = new createjs.
    Sprite(spriteSheet, "flap");
▸     animation.regX = 99;
▸     animation.regY = 58;
▸     animation.x = enemyXPos;
▸     animation.y = enemyYPos;
▸     animation.gotoAndPlay("flap");
▸     stage.addChildAt(animation,1);
▸   }
```

Example 10-13: The createEnemy() function.

```
▸     // Add ticker
▸     createjs.Ticker.setFPS(15);
▸     createjs.Ticker.addEventListener('tick',
    stage);
▸     createjs.Ticker.addEventListener('tick',
    tickEvent);
▸
▸     // Set up events AFTER the game is
    loaded
▸       window.onmousedown = handleMouseDown;
```

Example 10-14: The callback functions that fire the gun when the screen is tapped.

8 The spritesheet objects are used to create the object sprites that appear on the stage. I wrote a separate function called createEnemy() that handles this process, as shown in example 10-13.

The ticker code is used to set the speed of the animation occurring on the stage and to also fire a tickEvent() function that will be used to update various parts of the game interface.

9 In example 10-14, we also set the callback functions that deal with the user tapping the device screen to fire the gun.

10　　The tickEvent() callback function (shown in example 10-15) is used to adjust the speed and position of the enemy bat animation. The code first checks to make sure that the position of the enemy sprite is within the bounds of the game HEIGHT and WIDTH constants. If outside, it reverses the direction of the speed (separately along the X and Y axes) by multiplying its speed by -1. In essence, this reverses the direction of movement of the object. After the speed is altered or reversed as necessary, new X and Y coordinates are set for the sprite instance named animation.

```
function tickEvent()
{
    //Make sure enemy bat is within game
boundaries and move enemy Bat
    if(enemyXPos < WIDTH && enemyXPos > 0)
    {
        enemyXPos += enemyXSpeed;
    } else
    {
        enemyXSpeed = enemyXSpeed *
(-1);
        enemyXPos += enemyXSpeed;
    }
    if(enemyYPos < HEIGHT && enemyYPos > 0)
    {
        enemyYPos += enemyYSpeed;
    } else
    {
        enemyYSpeed = enemyYSpeed *
(-1);
        enemyYPos += enemyYSpeed;
    }

    animation.x = enemyXPos;
    animation.y = enemyYPos;
}
```

Example 10-15: The tickEvent() function.

11 The next function is really the heart of the game. In this function, I use a crude collision detection technique to see if the shot was within 40 pixels of the X and Y position of the enemy sprite. Note that the position of the sprite is returned as a floating point number, so Javascript's Math.round() function was used.

If, based on this technique, the user's shot was determined to be a hit, several things will happen. First, the enemy sprite will be removed from the stage and the batDeath() function called. This function runs the batDeath animation you saw earlier. The player score is incremented, a sound effect is played, and the speed of the enemy sprites is increased to make the game more difficult. The bitmap text for the score is updated at this point, as well.

After a random time increment of up to 3.5 seconds, a new instance of the enemy bat sprite is created and the game continues.

```javascript
function handleMouseDown(event)
{

  //Play Gunshot sound
  createjs.Sound.play("shot");

  //Increase speed of enemy slightly
  enemyXSpeed *= 1.05;
  enemyYSpeed *= 1.06;

  //Obtain Shot position
  var shotX = Math.round(event.clientX);
  var shotY = Math.round(event.clientY);
  var hitFlagX = false;
  var hitFlagY = false;

  //If shot came within 40 pixels on the X and Y set hit flag to true
  for(var x = -20; x < 21; x++)
  {
    if(shotX + x == Math.round(animation.x))
    {
        hitFlagX = true;
    }
  }
```

```
    if(shotY + x == Math.round(animation.y))
    {
            hitFlagY = true;
    }

}

    if(hitFlagY && hitFlagX)
    {
            //Hit
            stage.removeChild(animation);
            batDeath();
            score += 100;
            scoreText.text = "1UP: " + score.toString();
            createjs.Sound.play("deathSound");

    //Make it harder next time
            enemyYSpeed *= 1.25;
            enemyXSpeed *= 1.3;

            //Create new enemy
            var timeToCreate = Math.floor((Math.random()*3500)+1);
                    setTimeout(createEnemy,timeToCreate);

    } else
    {
            //Miss
            score -= 10;
            scoreText.text = "1UP: " + score.toString();

    }
```

Example 10-16: The heart of the game. Collision detection technique.

If the shot is determined to be a miss, 10 is subtracted from the player score and the new score bitmap is displayed.

```
function updateTime()
{
    gameTime += 1;
    if(gameTime > 60)
    {
            //End Game and Clean up
            timerText.text = "GAME OVER";
            stage.removeChild(animation);
            stage.removeChild(crossHair);
            var si =createjs.Sound.
play("gameOverSound");
            clearInterval(gameTimer);
    }
    else
    {
            timerText.text = "Time: " +
gameTime
   createjs.Sound.play("tick");
    }
}
```

Example 10-17: The updateTime() function.

12 You'll remember that during the game initialization process we started a Javascript timer that calls this updateTime() function each second.

This function increments the gameTime variable by 1. If the gameTime is greater than 60, the game is over, components are removed from the stage, and a "Game Over" sound effect is played.

Testing on a Device

Assuming your device is connected to your computer via USB cable and correctly provisioned (iOS only), you should be able to actually test on your device itself.

If you were testing on an Android device, you should be able to navigate to your project folder using the command line. Once pointed at the project folder, issue the following command:

```
phonegap build android
```

Or, to build on iOS:

```
phonegap build ios
```

If you have the Android SDK installed, you can also test on screen using an on-screen emulator. This can be very slow because the emulator is building a fully featured virtual Android device on top of your current operating system.

Congratulations! You've finished the game, this week's app, and the entire program! You should be proud of yourself and all you've accomplished.

We'll miss you!

The Full Code Listing

For your reference, here's the full code for the "Bat Hunt" app:

index.html

```html
<!DOCTYPE html>
<!--
   Copyright (c) 2012-2014 Adobe Systems Incorporated. All rights reserved.

   Licensed to the Apache Software Foundation (ASF) under one
   or more contributor license agreements. See the NOTICE file
   distributed with this work for additional information
   regarding copyright ownership. The ASF licenses this file
   to you under the Apache License, Version 2.0 (the
   "License"); you may not use this file except in compliance
   with the License. You may obtain a copy of the License at

   http://www.apache.org/licenses/LICENSE-2.0

   Unless required by applicable law or agreed to in writing,
   software distributed under the License is distributed on an
   "AS IS" BASIS, WITHOUT WARRANTIES OR CONDITIONS OF ANY
    KIND, either express or implied. See the License for the
   specific language governing permissions and limitations
   under the License.
-->
<html>
  <head>
    <meta charset="utf-8" />
    <meta name="format-detection" content="telephone=no" />
    <meta name="msapplication-tap-highlight" content="no" />
    <!-- WARNING: for iOS 7, remove the width=device-width and height=device-height
attributes. See https://issues.apache.org/jira/browse/CB-4323 -->
    <meta name="viewport" content="user-scalable=no, initial-scale=1, maximum-
scale=1, minimum-scale=1, width=device-width, height=device-height, target-
densitydpi=device-dpi" />
      <link href="normalize.css" type="text/css" rel="stylesheet" />
      <link href="game.css" type="text/css" rel="stylesheet" />
      <script language="javascript" type="text/javascript" src="http://code.createjs.
```

```
com/createjs-2013.12.12.min.js" ></script>
    <script language="javascript" type="text/javascript" src="fastclick.js"></
script>
    <script language="javascript" type="text/javascript" src="init.js" ></script>
    <script type="text/javascript" src="cordova.js"></script>
    <title>Bat Hunt</title>
  </head>
  <body>
    <canvas id="myCanvas"></canvas>
  </body>
</html>
```

Example 10-18: The full code listing for HTML "index" file.

init.js

```
var context;
var queue;
var WIDTH = 1024;
var HEIGHT = 768;
var batImage;
var stage;
var animation;
var deathAnimation;
var spriteSheet;
var enemyXPos=100;
var enemyYPos=100;
var enemyXSpeed = 1.5;
var enemyYSpeed = 1.75;
var score = 0;
var scoreText;
var gameTimer;
var gameTime = 0;
var timerText;

window.onload = function()
{
```

```
/*
 *   Set up the Canvas with Size and height
 *
 */
var canvas = document.getElementById('myCanvas');
context = canvas.getContext('2d');
context.canvas.width = WIDTH;
context.canvas.height = HEIGHT;
stage = new createjs.Stage("myCanvas");

/*
 *   Set up the Asset Queue and load sounds
 *
 */
queue = new createjs.LoadQueue(false);
queue.installPlugin(createjs.Sound);
queue.on("complete", queueLoaded, this);
createjs.Sound.alternateExtensions = ["ogg"];

/*
 *   Create a load manifest for all assets
 *
 */
queue.loadManifest([
  {id: 'backgroundImage', src: 'assets/background.png'},
  {id: 'crossHair', src: 'assets/crosshair.png'},
  {id: 'shot', src: 'assets/shot.mp3'},
  {id: 'background', src: 'assets/countryside.mp3'},
  {id: 'gameOverSound', src: 'assets/gameOver.mp3'},
  {id: 'tick', src: 'assets/tick.mp3'},
  {id: 'deathSound', src: 'assets/die.mp3'},
  {id: 'batSpritesheet', src: 'assets/batSpritesheet.png'},
  {id: 'batDeath', src: 'assets/batDeath.png'},
]);
queue.load();

/*
 *   Create a timer that updates once per second
 *
 */
gameTimer = setInterval(updateTime, 1000);
```

```
    }

    function queueLoaded(event)
    {
      // Add background image
      var backgroundImage = new createjs.Bitmap(queue.getResult("backgroundImage"))
      stage.addChild(backgroundImage);

      //Add Score
      scoreText = new createjs.Text("1UP: " + score.toString(), "36px Arial", "#FFF");
      scoreText.x = 10;
      scoreText.y = 10;
      stage.addChild(scoreText);

      //Ad Timer
      timerText = new createjs.Text("Time: " + gameTime.toString(), "36px Arial",
    "#FFF");
      timerText.x = 800;
      timerText.y = 10;
      stage.addChild(timerText);

      // Play background sound
      createjs.Sound.play("background", {loop: -1});

      // Create bat spritesheet
      spriteSheet = new createjs.SpriteSheet({
        "images": [queue.getResult('batSpritesheet')],
        "frames": {"width": 198, "height": 117},
        "animations": { "flap": [0,4] }
      });

      // Create bat death spritesheet
      batDeathSpriteSheet = new createjs.SpriteSheet({
        "images": [queue.getResult('batDeath')],
        "frames": {"width": 198, "height" : 148},
        "animations": {"die": [0,7, false,1 ] }
      });

      // Create bat sprite
      createEnemy();

      /*
```

```
    // Create crosshair
    crossHair = new createjs.Bitmap(queue.getResult("crossHair"));
    crossHair.x = WIDTH/2;
    crossHair.y = HEIGHT/2;
    stage.addChild(crossHair);
    */

    // Add ticker
    createjs.Ticker.setFPS(15);
    createjs.Ticker.addEventListener('tick', stage);
    createjs.Ticker.addEventListener('tick', tickEvent);

    // Set up events AFTER the game is loaded
    window.onmousedown = handleMouseDown;
}

function createEnemy()
{
    animation = new createjs.Sprite(spriteSheet, "flap");
    animation.regX = 99;
    animation.regY = 58;
    animation.x = enemyXPos;
    animation.y = enemyYPos;
    animation.gotoAndPlay("flap");
    stage.addChildAt(animation,1);
}

function batDeath()
{
  deathAnimation = new createjs.Sprite(batDeathSpriteSheet, "die");
  deathAnimation.regX = 99;
  deathAnimation.regY = 58;
  deathAnimation.x = enemyXPos;
  deathAnimation.y = enemyYPos;
  deathAnimation.gotoAndPlay("die");
  stage.addChild(deathAnimation);
}

function tickEvent()
{
    //Make sure enemy bat is within game boundaries and move enemy Bat
    if(enemyXPos < WIDTH && enemyXPos > 0)
```

```
        {
                enemyXPos += enemyXSpeed;
        } else
        {
                enemyXSpeed = enemyXSpeed * (-1);
                enemyXPos += enemyXSpeed;
        }
        if(enemyYPos < HEIGHT && enemyYPos > 0)
        {
                enemyYPos += enemyYSpeed;
        } else
        {
                enemyYSpeed = enemyYSpeed * (-1);
                enemyYPos += enemyYSpeed;
        }

    animation.x = enemyXPos;
    animation.y = enemyYPos;


  }


  function handleMouseDown(event)
  {

    //Display CrossHair
    crossHair = new createjs.Bitmap(queue.getResult("crossHair"));
    crossHair.x = event.clientX-45;
    crossHair.y = event.clientY-45;
    stage.addChild(crossHair);
    createjs.Tween.get(crossHair).to({alpha: 0},1000);

    //Play Gunshot sound
    createjs.Sound.play("shot");

    //Increase speed of enemy slightly
    enemyXSpeed *= 1.05;
    enemyYSpeed *= 1.06;

    //Obtain Shot position
    var shotX = Math.round(event.clientX);
```

```
var shotY = Math.round(event.clientY);
var spriteX = Math.round(animation.x);
var spriteY = Math.round(animation.y);

// Compute the X and Y distance using absolte value
var distX = Math.abs(shotX - spriteX);
var distY = Math.abs(shotY - spriteY);

// Anywhere in the body or head is a hit - but not the wings
if(distX < 30 && distY < 59 )
{
  //Hit
  stage.removeChild(animation);
  batDeath();
  score += 100;
  scoreText.text = "1UP: " + score.toString();
  createjs.Sound.play("deathSound");

   //Make it harder next time
  enemyYSpeed *= 1.25;
  enemyXSpeed *= 1.3;

  //Create new enemy
  var timeToCreate = Math.floor((Math.random()*3500)+1);
    setTimeout(createEnemy,timeToCreate);

} else
{
  //Miss
  score -= 10;
  scoreText.text = "1UP: " + score.toString();

}
}

function updateTime()
{
  gameTime += 1;
  if(gameTime > 60)
  {
        //End Game and Clean up
        timerText.text = "GAME OVER";
```

```
            stage.removeChild(animation);
            stage.removeChild(crossHair);
    createjs.Sound.removeSound("background");
    var si =createjs.Sound.play("gameOverSound");
            clearInterval(gameTimer);
    }
    else
    {
            timerText.text = "Time: " + gameTime
    createjs.Sound.play("tick");
    }
}
```

Example 10-19: The full code listing for the Javascript "init" file.

Congratulations! You've come a long way since you first opened this book, haven't you? You're now able to control video and audio, parse both XML and JSON, and you've even gained some experience with gaming techniques! The new skills you've adopted and refined throughout this book will help you in all sorts of future projects.

If you enjoyed this book and want to learn a little more about what goes into making these apps, we have a program that takes an even more in-depth look at the processes. Our **10 Apps in 10 Weeks** course gives you access to all the elements you need, including music files, icons for mobile, splash screens, and the complete finalized code.   There's also a handy comment section where you can chat with your peers and even ask for help if you hit a snag.

(You can find a coupon for a bundle--which includes this program AND our **Mobile App Development with HTML5** program--at the beginning of the book!)

You should be proud of yourself and all you've accomplished! There is so much you can do with your new skills. Good luck on the rest of your programming journey, no matter what direction you decide to take.